NOTUNOL

A Study of Christism

By

Mac R. Cabanilla

Inks and Bindings
888-290-5218
www.inksandbindings.com
orders@inksandbindings.com

Dedication

In memory of our late father Godofredo R. Cabanilla Sr., a firm advocate of the message of justification by faith in Christianity.

CONTENTS

THE STRUCTURE OF MORALITY

THE PRESERVATION OF ALL LIVING ORGANISIMS COMPLETELY DEPENDS UPON THE faithful observance of the structure of morality inherently provided by Creator or God. Without it, the continuity of a species couldn't progress, and a random new emergence of difference species of life forms should have been very prevalent at any given time in history, including the present. But it's undoubtedly evident that most, if not all, species or life forms existing at the present time have had a long, established genealogy.

The American Heritage dictionary defines *morality* as the quality of being in accord with standards of right or good conduct, a virtuous conduct. Sociologically this is a very generalized interpretation of morality. In this study of the structure of morality, morality should have the meaning of the responsibility for the preservation of life of any species by itself or in symbiosis with respect to necessity and with its full environment. The structure of morality is not provided necessarily in anticipation of the possibility of sin, or, even if it is the case, it shouldn't have much impact on the main objective of this study. Competition is not evil, but it's the method of competition that developed as the violation of the structure of morality before it had the chance to reach its full structure as the evidence that immortality either denied along the way or delayed reaching its appointed time.

Morality is structured with these five dynamic forces:
1. **Self-preservation and cell division**. A cell division is equivalent with marriage in human beings and copulation in other life forms, although cell division is a fundamental operation in all life forms including human beings.
2. **Altruism and acquiescence.**
3. **Conscience and power of choice (freedom).**
4. **Faith and hope.**
5. **Righteousness and immorality.**

Self-preservation and cell division as the first part of the structure of morality is present to all life forms on earth and probably even in a universal magnitude. Bacteria and viruses, the smallest organisms, have the instinct to compete for nourishment for survival and exhibit the act of cell division for the sole purpose of perpetuating their species. Even plants do strive to compete for the energy of the sun when something, from any structure or from among other plants, is obstructing their free access to it. Because bacteria and viruses are microorganisms with a simple life form or structure, they don't possess the other structures of morality. Their requirements or needs for their survival are very simple; some bacteria could even manufacture all of their basic needs just by the presence of carbon dioxide, nitrogen, and air. The anaerobic bacteria don't even require the presence of air elemental oxygen for their survival; they can extract it from their food. Plants are a little higher form of life than bacteria because some of them do need some form of sexual activity; for example, the existence of male and female, but some plants have self-pollination mechanism. Actually, bacteria and plants, or mostly all life forms, have a symbiotic affinity with beneficial bacteria. This symbiotic principle indicates a general purpose of creation, and it seems that life has a noble purpose with or without the existence of deadly pathogens.

The second structure of morality, altruism and acquiescence, is present in most higher life forms, except as previously stated with bacteria and viruses. It may be present a little with bacteria due to the symbiosis principle. Some animals do exhibit altruism in the fact that they, like the chicken and the pig, actually could live in the same barn without physically harming one another or trying to struggle for food against one another. In fact, a lot of animals of different species could cohabitate or live in this situation. Undoubtedly, acquiescence is exhibited in most animals in parental care but sometimes even with other animals. Human beings shouldn't be classified as belonging to the animal kingdom because of its unique and very complex form of existence in terms of intelligence and lifestyles. Regardless that the human cell resembles the rest of life forms, it's only because of the unified theory of creation and the existence of only one creator.

If altruism wasn't available in the early history of human beings, perhaps we couldn't have come this far as a very modernized and intelligent civilization. However even if this modern human civilization is as materially appealing as it seems, the trend has come to a point where the structure of morality starts to break apart. Even if few human beings have reached the most glorious pinnacle of material success, it is only obvious that morality has poised a downfall. Whether we like it or not, we owe a lot of things to the altruism of our ancestors; that is the very reason that we now celebrate honest heroes, idealists, philosophers, inventors, and others of the past who weren't motivated by anything else but the imperative and exigent demand of their time.

The third structure of morality is not proprietary or exclusive to human beings. Animals also exercise the power of choice in the way they select their mates. There is even a little insinuation of the use of conscience because animals also possess a sense of right and wrong, but not as the human does. Just like altruism and acquiescence, conscience and the power of choice are inseparable forces of morality. The basis of this argument is: where is the valid origin of the value or the perception of conscience if all action is coerced? The idea of wrong actions, therefore, shouldn't have any pre-existence if is has no purpose; like the idea of the perception of right behavior, pre-existence must be predicated by its purpose. Or if the wrongness of an action is based only upon the proprietary aspect of another, then there's no objectivity of power. One behavior might be wrong by the concept of one person but permitted and cherished by another. Therefore, choice should be exercised to meet the demand of morality and fairness, but only on the basis that such disputable actions or behaviors don't inflict harm to another. Even the affirmative value of the action of the rightness of a behavior or action, if the availability of the power of choice is not present, it couldn't possibly be executed. The nature of perception is the function of the power of choice. Everything that is perceived must be evaluated to avoid catastrophe or bad action, like falling from a cliff or why a man doesn't eat a rock or soil. But if one is coerced – by the power of another - to eat a rock, then the product or result of another's perception has been abolished by the perception of the power of another. All the parts of the structure of morality are intended by the creator for the sole purpose of the preservation of life. Inherent, therefore, to all life forms is the possession of a degree of right and wrong or conscience, regardless that the power of choice may not be available or imparted to all life forms.

In fact, the greatest controversy that divided the social management mechanics or human beings between that of socialism and democratic form of governments lies on what part of the structure of morality dominates. In socialism, altruism might have been the overriding force that inspired or motivated its leaders or proponents. While in democratic forms of governments it's the freedom of choice that primarily became the dominant consideration of its founders. Actually, altruism as a positive force is only a subpart of conscience, regardless of its unavoidable necessity. It's the very reason that God installed conscience and power of choice to enhance the goodness of altruism. Because, regardless of the good intent of kindness, no one and nobody should be forced to do it; nobody should be forced to wear clothes without the individual free will of consent. So definitely altruism lacks another dimension required for the stability of life's interactions or civilization in general and, collaterally, of the unavoidable ascent of intelligence. The aforementioned is the obvious deficiency of socialism. It must be observed and acknowledged that its part of the structure of morality is the basis and foundation of another from the very basic to the most complex. It must be noted that a democratic form of government is acknowledged within the structure of morality as a higher standard of social management; it must be understood that conscience, in order to uphold itself with the highest of virtue, its mechanism, and dynamic, must continue to preserve and not disregard the third structure of morality.

The fourth structure of morality as faith and hope is itself self-explanatory. Though it seems simple, it involves some complexity. Faith could only be exercised by an organism or life form with a higher sense of purpose. This dimension of the structure of morality is only available to the highest form of life, and that is the human being. This response mechanism, or actions and decisions, is what actually separates the unique and special status of human beings from the rest of the other life forms. Although faith has only two components, its usage and utility are quite too complicated for the grasp of lower forms of life; therefore, it's only awarded and given to human beings who have a large capacity of intelligence.

Faith is derived by the understanding and perception of both the spiritual and physical realms of existence. It's in faith where the concept and idea of religion and belief of the existence of God lies. Religion, unlike the proponents of the study of physics and related sciences, confronts instead of avoids or entertains the mysteries or unexplained phenomena or existence. In Christian religion, faith has received considerable attention in regard to its usage and purpose; for example: "faith without works is dead," and "faith is the eye of things unseen." Faith is, relatively speaking, a relationship between a human being and his God and, on the same token, such a relationship itself lends its objective to a balanced relationship to all the rest of life (the consideration of evil and deadly pathogens is presented and discussed somewhere in Christism).

Hope is the result of faith, or faith predisposes hope. Faith is the reason and cause of hope. The ultimate goal of hope is immortality. But of what immortality? Of the spirit or of the flesh only or of both? It must be both; the immortality of the soul. Soul must be defined as the union of flesh and spirit. If immortality is only to be awarded to the spirit, then all physical existence, including the universe, is but a one-time event of temporal purpose as expressed by the coming of the next big bang of which origin was a random chance – or even if the big bang is cyclical, the theory of evolution of the origin of the species is also a random act of chance.

Righteousness and Immortality as the Fifth Structure of Morality

Righteousness is obtained or exercised when all the preceding parts and levels of the structure of morality are observed. In a way, therefore, even microorganisms which, if only by instinct, live a life within the level of morality and possess righteousness, regardless of the fact that the act of faith may be unknown by them. Righteousness is the observance of a right relationship within and among organisms or life forms; it's the act of objective life behavior in relation to oneself and to all created physical existence whether local and/or universal; it's standard action or decision or perception that has its object or ultimate goal as the preservation of one's life and all life or existence in general.

immortality is the only remaining part of the structure of morality that has been either denied because sin sets in before its endowment or its appointed time has been delayed. The Jewish scripture stipulated that immortality had been taken away from Adam and Eve because of sin. Because the Jewish scripture only revolves its principles and beliefs within itself, it couldn't be completely regarded as an altogether objective source of absolute truth, because truth must acknowledge physical realities and natural laws, a physical reality that God himself created. But it's not the objective of this study of the structure of morality to disprove the Jewish scripture because it has its rights and privileges to posit its own ideals and concepts of the nature of reality, and the truth must always be accepted or rejected by the scrutiny of the (individual) aspect and perceptions of the most honest seekers of absolute truth.

If immortality has not reached its appointed time, then creation may not be finished. Regardless, along the way in the process of ongoing creation, sin occurred. It's because each level and part of the structure of morality is actually a prerequisite of another, and the process couldn't properly continue its ascent to exact completion until the demands of each level and parts were met or satisfied. In view of further analysis, sin and deficiencies of organisms in the evolutionary process in a supposed rapid progression must have played a great part in delaying the full development and completion of the structure of morality. But if the creation was finished and immortality was to be imparted or rewarded to those individuals who gained righteousness as a future event of salvation, even in such a case a tremendous and extensive change must be made with the existing natural laws of all physical existence to accommodate the nature of the physical existence of immortality. In this regard, the aging process must be completely revised and will completely repel the idea of a catastrophic proposition of a black hole and the Big Bang.

No matter what way or in what point of time the reward of immortality will come, the opinion that is must definitely come must be argued. The details of this argument are discussed in Christism because the main objective of this short study is confined to presenting the full structure of morality. It must be understood that all the rest and

7

branches of human behavior have their roots in the structure of morality. The first structure of morality alone comprises enormous branches of human activities and behavior. Books and volumes of documents could be written about the act of courtship and marriage alone - as culture developed in complexity - as a part of the first structure of morality in the modern society.

Summary: For the full understanding of the necessity of the structure of morality and achievement of its full benefit one must have a good understanding of the study and proposition of Christism as the unified theory of existence or the universe. Because in Christism the cause and object of faith is derived. However, it's necessary to illustrate that the structure of morality could actually be divided into two dynamic relationships. From the first part of the structure of morality of self-preservation to the third level of conscience and freedom could constitute the first division as a dynamic force which defines the relationship of an organism to himself (itself) and to other organism(s). The second division of the structure of morality could start with faith and reach immortality, which defines the relationships of the human being to his creator or God. And because human being alone is capable of exercising or understanding the meaning and value of faith, all the rest of creation would not be obligated to participate in obtaining their immortality. All living organism(s) below human beings would automatically receive immortality when it comes or when it will be rewarded.

Because of the unique nature and intelligence of human beings, they are the only living organisms that are obligated to fulfill a dual duty or responsibility to obtain immortality. Righteousness is an obligation of all human beings for the preservation of self and the responsibility to other life forms. But such righteousness doesn't exactly warrant an automatic reward of immortality without the act or consciousness of having faith in his creator. Righteousness without faith means that an individual has no priority or wish for immortality. All concepts and ideas of eternal life or immortality only come through a belief in God or purpose, so only faith is mandatory for salvation. In Christian scripture, Apostle Paul emphasized that a man is justified by faith. While on the other hand, Saint James asserts that faith without works is dead. Both of these declarations are correct, for faith inspires good works or righteousness, and what is righteous is man's duty to himself and to others. Faith is a belief in God. So, faith and righteousness are in correspondence: meaning that when an individual believes in God, it motivates him or her to do good works to oneself and to others. When righteousness abounds, faith fortified, so is one's hope for immortality. (Read Christism for the full understanding of faith.)

Perhaps it's not just a coincidence that the structure of morality depicts the purpose of God. The Christian Bible itself declares: "I am the Alpha and Omega" (Rev. 1:8); this means that God created life and provides immortality. The creation of life is very much the expression of the first structure of morality, which is self-preservation (a spiritual response mechanism) and cell division (a pure physical activity), and the last structure of morality expresses a similar purpose that righteousness is a spiritual (mind) and physical (immortality) reality.

ORIGIN: FAITH

THE SEARCH FOR THE ABSOLUTE TRUTH (CHRISTISM). THE PROPOSITION OF CHRISTISM ON the enigma of origin. Theory of the absolute in relation to the very existence of God.

This is not a scientific study. It's not recommended to those who have a fear of losing one's allegiance to a specific religious faith or belief system. Read further at your own risks or benefits.

Warning: The individual must be completely responsible for any outcome/result of his/her own action, response, or understanding in reading the contents of this book. It may convince you to honestly believe in the existence of God or may change/abandon your religion or belief system.

A layman's proposition of salvation by faith:

if the only two entities in universal existence which presuppose an absolute existence of eternity are space and time, then the question is: how could something (matter) deal with its ultimate proposition of immortality?

Time and space are two inseparable and immortal entities in all universal phenomena. They are the basis of all existence even if they don't necessarily possess an accountable physical reality. They are immortal on the basis that they don't necessarily require any other being or entities for their existence neither that they could be eliminated by virtue of any accountability or non-accountability of/to another. Unlike with the structure of accounting (spirit), it requires the deliberate, or otherwise, interaction of two beings or things. Accounting or spirit, therefore, is the third reality that is indispensable or inherently has the intrigue of the possession of immortality.

The best position of accounting is that it precedes the existence of structured matter or energy philosophically or mathematically. And in relation to the origin of matter, accounting and origin of matter coexisted in the likeness of the relationship of time and space. It could be decided that accounting is in the very spirit of the existence of matter, for without it wisdom and knowledge couldn't proceed further, such that atomic structures couldn't possibly be created nor could any thought process of creation be made viable. Accounting should not only be literally understood as a judgment or reckoning of arithmetic or mathematics. It should also comprise the component of symmetry and pictorial dimensions, so structures of energy levels could be appropriated even without dealing with direct numeral values.

The dilemma of the existence of God the son (matter) is predisposed upon its need of revelation to himself and all other creations; it's the very expression that God the father (nothing) has reason to be jealous. This is the factor of the plan and origin of all colors in the universal reality. Likewise, the dilemma of matters. Therefore, the cycles of life and all decay and regeneration or recreation of all matter is a very clear and obvious assertion of the immortal quest of the processes or holy spirit of God (accounting). God the son, or matter, thereby is relative in its immortal existence even with the full consideration of its mercantile or usable value. In order for accounting (spirit) to possess immortality (which is relative) the forms of all matter must undergo changes in form, shape, or size while retaining its character or species. This is the theory of energy that couldn't be created or destroyed, or the first law of thermodynamics.

Regardless of the relative immortality of God the son (matter) and the spirit (accounting), it inherently could possess the absolute immortality of time and space (the nothing) due to their benign and innocuous interactions which require no loss of energy but exchanges actions or interactions, although God the son (matter) and the spirit are the major benefactors of the activity. The constant interactions of these two entities explains all the universal causation of eternal motions and therefore is the basis of all life forms, creation and recreation, and universal motions.

The ultimate expression of the immortal quest of the attribute of God's immortality, at least that which is required to redeem God's virtue in our system, is the revelation of Christ (matter) which symbolizes God's physical immortality and righteousness. This righteousness of God is exacting, which, however, doesn't completely divulge that God is not compromising because of God the son's (matter) relative absolute immortality. Compromising, forgiving, and the related attributes of God shouldn't be confused with the exacting demand of mathematical or philosophical accounting attributes of the spirit.

The very basic infrastructures of nature of absolute theory of reality are the basis of all complex forms of existence. The limited scope of physical sciences which could only deal with the examination of matters couldn't in any way participate in the study of things that aren't seen and which have no physical realities regardless of the fact that they have an absolute existence. Time, for example, has been measured - at least at some argument - but it has no physical reality because if time is a particle, then we could stop and manipulate its elements. The accounting of time is not limited to mechanical motions between two points or to a steady state of matter at one point, because infinite time exists in the infinite span of space.

Regardless, this very basic infrastructure of all universal existence means that all existence only requires these three entities of universal phenomena: space and time, matter, and accounting (spirit of the universe). These are the only three possible structures of existence, locally or universally. To issue validity to this argument, one has to understand the coexistence of time and space. Every time that time is considered, the element of space must also be considered regardless of whether any matter is present or not; however, its essence and value are only to be appreciated by the spirit of matter or form. The word *accounting* being substituted for the spirit of God or matter is primarily done for the reason of the broad use of the word. The word *spirit* is very limited in scope, and a mysterious universe deserves a broader word to define its operations – even beyond the meaning of words: *logic, intelligence, philosophy,* and so on.

There are no other dimensions of universal existence besides the aforementioned. The consideration of power (political, religious, social, etc., evil, greed, morality, virtue, etc.) are all responsibilities of accountability, and all other human spiritual behavior considered evil or moral is discussed under the structure of morality (see Structure of Morality) which is a study of consideration not limited to spirituality but with full material indications and/or derivatives/objectives.

The Nature of the Force of Space (Nothing)

There's no possible and rational way of avoiding the crux of the existence of the infinite nature of space, or nothing, which at the same time has magnitude and force far greater than the totality of the universal mass/weight, not unless there's an acceptable, rational evidence of the existence of an infinite mass of the universe so that not to admit or disregard that the emptiness of space alone carries the universe in its place. This phenomenon couldn't be stipulated in terms of any physical arguments of measurements for its nature is strictly theoretical/philosophical or spiritual. To attempt to question the validity of the existence of the force of space, or nothing, the question of the origin of matter/energy itself must likewise be proven beforehand. Like time, the existence of space is not limited between two points of energies.

There are only two possible theoretical arguments as to how a tremendously heavy universal mass of energy behaves in space. The first assumption is a wandering universe: a free-falling, universal, huge mass delving into the infinite deep of nothing that has no force or buoyancy. The other is a stationary universe (though it has motions within itself) that is suspended by the force of the nothing or void. The former is very improbable due to the heavy mass of the universe, and if the void has no buoyancy, then the speed of motion couldn't possibly sustain life or would produce a chaotic condition, but even if it could manage organization, the huge consumption of energy could have ended the life (material form) of the universe very quickly. The latter theory that there is a force of nothing which has a value greater than the total universal mass is the more logical explanation of the existence of the universe which has a limited or finite mass.

The Nature of Time

The consideration of time doesn't always necessarily derive its value upon the accounting or reckoning of another. Human beings didn't invent the accounting of time, it's been inherent in nature even before the existence of anything, and it was an indispensable element in creation, but intelligent beings had witnessed the presence of time such as the motions of matter between distances or how long matter has been in its place. If intelligence invented time by an accounting of physical reality alone, then we could assume that all existence or form is just by reckoning or accounting and thereby has the ability to deny all immaterial things and the creation of a time machine to recreate past realities of life would be feasible because physical realities come into existence by assumption (see The Truth and Mathematics).

The origin of time wasn't in itself a creation of the expansion of the theoretical Big Bang, regardless of the fact that time is an integral part of all existence. Time has a preexistence with the infinity of the preexistence of space before the assumed Big Bang, of which a theory has limited its concept of space and time between points or energy, but in reality it's not the case.

The Nature of God in Religious School of Thoughts

In the Judeo-Christian Scripture (Bible) from Genesis to the book of Revelation, the meaning of the worship and human interaction with God is unavoidably noticeable. In the book of Genesis, it is stipulated that God is the creator (of all things), and concurrently, the same God is the provider of all the immediate needs of humanity. And in the history of the people who wrote it, the same God was their continual source of guidance and comfort in their personal, social, and religious experiences. This huge religious system culminated with the monumental belief that God in the person of Christ became the redeemer and promise of immortality. The idea that the "word was made flesh" (John 1:14) is an ideology that not only depicts a pure religious ambition, but, as mysterious as it may seem, it also relates to something beyond religious understanding. The period of the belief of Christ is a dilemma not easily reconcilable to extinction to those who don't believe in God because of its affinity to the modern age in which Christian followers still dominate in worldwide proportion, and also by the sustainable proposition of material evidence presented and the sustainable, ever-present, unexplained nature of the universe.

Mostly a lot of religious practitioners believe in the existence of a personal divine being, who possesses extraordinary powers expressed in Judeo-Christian Scripture as omniscient, omnipresent, and omnipotent. But the mean objectives and purposes of such a belief in God–whether they be of those who worship the sun, volcano, fire, wind, tree, or what have they–is that God is the creator, provider, and comforter in times of trouble; a physician who gives healing from all diseases and maladies; and most of all who offers the faith of immortality.

In most, if not all, religious belief systems, God is a spirit which could mysteriously assume any physical form upon his demand or discretion at any time. The same God could inspire or motivate the mind or spirit of man through mysterious pure spiritual mediums of either direct or indirect fashions. The Jewish or Christian scriptures are believed to have been written through the direct inspiration of God. Regardless of any religious faith, belief, or speculation, the burden of proof or the recognition of the truth should be left as the individual believer's options alone, according to one's experiences, encounters, or perceptions of reality.

The Origin of Matter in Physical Science Standpoint

Physical scientist study and think about energy/matter in a very different reality by denying the existence of God or by accepting either a separate or complete non-existence. In science the origin of matter came by way of accidental episodes called the Big Bang–a big bang which has no credible explanation of its origin, a scientific myth that offers that there's no ultimate purpose behind all forms and activities, universally or locally. This motive or decision is not unpredictable for there will be no answer to the question of the origin of how energy existed even at the full considerations of physical sciences. The only viable pursuit is how close our understanding can come to, or whose philosophical wisdom has more affinity to the mystery of things, or whose knowledge is most admissible to one's honest perceptive mind searching for the absolute truth.

In physics there are brilliant theories which end with evidence of actual realities (an atomic explosion) that seem to suggest that the origin and formation of atoms was caused by the tremendous contraction of implosion of universal force from the formation of a dense soup or mixture of subatomic particles in the beginning of time after the Big

Bang. The theory of general relativity suggests that space is created by the force of expansion, and because space and motions were created time came into being. The energy and mass of a light-emitting point or object could be known from the aspect of another point receiving a light. Also, the distance between two points could be known as long as a relationship existed by which one object or point was emitting light and the other was receiving. Because all human understanding of the universe if fundamentally from the aspect or point of view of the planet Earth, all observations and measurements in attempting to understand the universe must start from the full understanding of the nature of the planet Earth (gravitational force, etc.) and the light that it receives from other objects of the universe.

Physics has produced the theory of general relativity which mathematically calculated the whole mass of the universe. But the theory seemed to be deficient and as not reliable as an absolute explanation of the nature of universe because its stipulation expressed that all space could be contracted into singularity, but even such a singularity might have occupied a space and couldn't possible hold its own weight at the same time. This singularity exploded and created the universal space and time between galaxies, or in general between points or objects. The theory of the Big Bang or general relativity is limited as an opinion of the aspect within the universe; therefore, the universe has no edge and will continually expand with an infinite mass. Because physics excluded the notion of any purpose of creation, there is no God but that the theory of general relativity and the Big Bang is the creator or origin of the universal existence. Probably the biggest setback of the theory of the Big Bang is its proposition that the singularity didn't necessarily need an outside force to have sustained or aided such a massive force of contraction in the formation of universal existence, and by an unknown origin of a huge gravitational force in the contraction of a black hole, which itself is believed into complete non-existence. As in religion, science is not without abundant myths.

An Alternative Theory of the Origin of the Universe

Directly contradictory to the Big Bang and singulary theory of the origin of the universe is the unified theory of existence which stipulates that time and space and energy preexisted at the same time before the creation of the material universe. In the beginning of time the universe is mostly an infinite span of space, but it wasn't completely void of energy. Regardless that the zero force is predominant, it contains ripple amounts of energy (not limited with the definition of motion between time and space). On one side is the positive energy (and its rudimentary particles), and on another is the negative force (and its rudimentary parts). Positive energy is only a force acting in a different way from the negative as well as from the zero force. Likewise, negative energy is only a force acting in a different fashion against another force which has the tendency to attract the positive force and repel its own kind. So is the huge zero force; it behaves completely differently from all other forces.

In the beginning, before the creation of matter or the physical universe, the ripple amounts of energy were present and diffused throughout the huge infinite span of space. Because, unlike physics, which completely disregarded any purpose of creation but by a sole random chance, the problem whether the ripple energy in space was diffused uniformly of the different atomic structures. Contradictory to physics, the creation of the universe started with a purpose, so that when the totality of the span of space expanded, the ripple energy of subatomic, positive, and negative forces was released or shaken off as free elements, as protons, electrons, plasmas, gases, etc. Through the further action of the space expansion (that cannot expand but to contract) the free electrons and protons began to unite to form a nucleus of atoms instantaneous atomic energy structures. This action was possible by the expansive force of space concurrent with the pull of force created by the uniting elements which resulted in contraction or compression (this theory explains why all created objects a spherical). The combined strength of these forces

19

was calculated by a purpose so that specifications were actually employed that determined the creation of various forms of atomic structures and, subsequently, the installation and placement of the exact space between objects of the universe and the exact strategic locations for the creation of life through the action of gravitational forces. Because the act of creation is through and by the compression and contraction that was triggered by the space expansion, the degree of such forces applied in specific requirements created the need of specific locations. One example of this is the formation of water on planet Earth as the solar system is a composite of just one purpose; analogous to the specific designations of atoms in a particular purpose of an amino acid.

The tremendous amount of energy needed for the creation of the universe was the result of the simultaneous expansion of space and the pull of energy created from the fusion of proton and electron in the formation of the nucleus of the atom. Before that act of creation was initiated, the infinite span of universal space was completely filled and dominated by zero forces, but attached to the zero forces were ripple-diffused amounts of energy of subatomic particles, protons, and electrons, probably at designated or specified intervals or locations, so that two separate intelligences or spirits were actually present which devised the material or physical universal creation for the purpose of the creation of life, human beings, and other life forms. Since space had unloaded all of its energy to attend to a state of complete void or nothingness for the purpose of buoyancy to hold the universe in place, much of the free electrons and protons were left to remain free (as plasma) as the purpose for the creation of matter exceeded its needs even after the creation of various massive objects in the universe that received considerable amounts of energy were given the nature to give off light by the energy particles and electromagnetic waves radiating back. One of these light-emitting objects, like the sun in the solar system, is an intended agent for the creation of life on planet Earth.

After the creation of the universe, the space became a cold vacuum, thereby completely attaining a state of an absolute zero force that had no mass and energy structure whatsoever but possessed strength that couldn't be measured in terms of energy by any energy structure or organism. Because the universe is created within the infinite span of space with an absolute zero buoyancy force, it is holding the universal mass it had created. Because space or the void remained within and without with all created forms, it has retained its life and spirit just like before the creation only that in the new order the something or matter or the ripple energy transformed its form into what we have now: a beautiful universe that created life and other intelligent beings with it, like human beings, in the solar system.

It must be fully understood for the sake of reason and reality that the nature of nothing or space, regardless that is has a force, is has no mass, neither has any energy structures; therefore, only space can declare absolute nature of infinity. The force of nothing or the void doesn't occupy space because it's the space; neither does it have a mass, but rather its sole purpose is to hold and accommodate mass or matter but is no longer physically reactive (in terms of energy consumption) to them but just simply holds them in place or position for the provision of motions. And, as we all know, without space there would be no motion, and if there's no motion there is no energy that could create life. Energy creates motion and motion creates energy because matter or energy must occupy a space. The nature of nothing or space (not just space limited between points) is a mystery that science couldn't prove or disprove, nor could anyone understand it, but anyone could believe according to reason and wisdom of faith and purpose.

It is very important to understand that the process of how the Big Bang happened wasn't possible in terms of reason and logic because, unlike the alleged contraction of the sun, the theoretical contraction has a physical container within the sun itself to have contained the compression force that is believed to have triggered a nuclear reaction explosion. The

Big Bang theory is only a unilateral understanding within the aspect of an observer within the physical or material universe. It is very important that one is to be able to contrast the diametrically opposed theories between the Big Bang and the unified theory or concept of the nature of existence or universe or God, in order for an individual to be able to have a clear choice about whether there's God or no God.

In any study of physical realities or matter there will always be a means for mathematical measurements to assume the age of the physical universe within the reach of one's observation, because any matter that has energy structures could be observed by other energy structures. So, therefore, one's perceptions and observations are one's truth in their own right. Knowledge is thereby a factor of observation but is has no relevance to effect that perception is absolute reality regardless of the fact that reality is perception. All knowledge, wisdom, perceptions, etc., are nothing but an interaction or accounting between energy structures; one such incidence is a human observing his universe. To issue a validity of the argument of the relationship of reality and perception, reality is directly proportional to creation and inversely proportional to perception so that creation or origin is the factor of reality (matter) and perception/knowledge, or etc. (spirit of creation or innovation). Perception or knowledge is utilized by god in creating the physical universe by the transformation of themselves. In a similar manner, man can utilize perception for inventions, but inventions have no inherent relevance to the creation of matter; it's only the transformation of matter from one purpose to another. One instance of man's innovation is the use of carbon molecules (organic chemistry) to form various products of industry, and yet carbon itself is a primary element of God's creation, especially life on Earth.

Since the knowledge of man has derived the age of the universe, it has declared a hypothetical truth to himself that the universe is finite in its mass and destiny, thereby reality/matter has no immortality according to physical science. But such an assumption of truth defies the relevance of an ever-expanding universe. The black hole and Big Bang theories are derived from the theory of general relativity of mathematical calculation based upon the accounting or observation of space and time that has existed between points or objects or between two energy levels or structures among themselves.

Even if all human knowledge of truth is to be limitedly construed to the accounting or perception within the universe or between points, and even if the mathematical calculation of the general relativity is correct, the origin of the things calculated must remain the overriding determinant for the admission of absolute truth. It's no wonder that the theory of general relativity must have an origin of singularity or contraction of all space in the beginning so that expansion became only a perception of space; therefore, the Big Bang is the origin. The notion of an ever-expanding universe is nothing but an empty assumption to issue relevance for the sole exigency or purpose to satisfy the idea that the physical universe must be holding itself. If the assumption (that energy/mass could be destroyed into eternal oblivion) of the black hole (energy consuming) does exist, then it violates the law of the conservation of energy and, of course, reason and purpose.

The nature that God had created has intended an accommodation of law of the conservation of energy. One of these is how planet Earth's atmosphere is protected from any escape of water vapor molecules existing its system. But in the universal domain of the infinity of space, its nothingness serves as a border for the conservation of universal energy as well as to provide support for the universal mass to stay in one location and its structure as one dynamic universal entity.

Regardless of the fact that science has produced a theoretical age of the universe, the relevance of such an assumption must be limited and relative only within the present capacity of the proposition. But with respect to logic and philosophical considerations, the universe indeed must have a finite mass and boundary. But to what extent the definition of the definite universal mass couldn't possibly be absolutely know by human technology alone. However, the fact that the universe has a finite mass doesn't necessarily impose an impending death of the universe. Regardless of the assumption of the general relativity expressed in alleged incidents of black holes and the Big Bang, the fact that the universe has an edge and finite mass is an absolute statement that the universe could sustain immortality as expressed in the theory of the unified nature of existence or the universe which mainly stipulates that the physical universal mass is within the infinite space (nothing) that is holding it regardless that they have interactions they don't actually exactly exhibit any form of bonding, fusion, or any actual transfer of energy between them. The nature of both space (nothing) and the physical universal mass of which, according to the purpose of creation, the created and will sustain the principle of the first law of

thermodynamics for the conservation of energy, regardless that the energy within the universal mass it permits the exercise of the laws of the second and third law of thermodynamics. By the purpose of creation, the nature of space became absolutely without mass; thereby even its cold or vacuum couldn't possibly accept heat transfer or exchange from the physical universe; neither could it exhibit energy transformation within itself, and this condition permits the possibility of energy conservation between the space (void) and the physical universe regardless that they constantly interact but without energy loss or gain from one to another. And this proposes eternal motion and causation for the ultimate probability of the immortality of the universe.

If the inquisition of the temptation whether the unified theory of existence or universe or God could provide an absolute basis of truth holds that the faith and hope of its proponents is relevant only upon how much proposition of absolute (alleged) truth of other theories or studies present. Therefore, any inquiry as to the full reliability of the unified theory of existence or universe or God, one must understand the relationship between reality and perception. The definition of reality must constitute all created matter or physical existence, while the definition of perception must include all theories, knowledge, understanding, and especially the ability of spirits or the spirit itself. Since the unified theory or existence is a concept or a perception, all of its values and veritableness, therefore, are relative to reality or physical existence. The formula *reality=origin (creation)/perception* will establish the full relationship with regard to the relativity of perception or spirit to the other two dynamic forces of existence, so that all spirit or perceptions are relative to both origin (creation) and matter. Even the spirit of God is relative to its existence in matter; likewise, the spirit of God the Father relates its existence to the zero mass of nothing. In summary, the unified theory of existence or universe or God completely relies on the probability of the existence of the nature of space, void, or nothing as discussed.

It would be hard to reconcile the unified theory of existence or God with any study of physical sciences due to the very nature of space or the nothing. But any objective or reliable pursuit of physical scientific studies should be, by all means, respected and worthy of all considerations of its merits. And in the same token, all spiritual, philosophical, or theoretical inquisition or presentation as to the nature of existence must not be physically abrogated by any scientific speculations due to what remains a mysterious origin of energy or matter in general, even from the aspect of physical sciences; however, all speculations or perceptions as to the origin and nature of universal existence or God must be theoretically adjudged or justified by the sole perception and discretion of the honest seeker of truth relevant to the proximity of the absolute rationality or wisdom. Relevance to this notion equates that the reality of any believer of a faith is a perception of the origin of the universe or matter. In a specific instance, a Christian reality is distinct from an Evolutionist reality of the perception or belief in the creation or the origin of the universe. It's, therefore, definitive that perception is not a sense of general reality but rather only relative to a specific faith or religion or philosophy. But reality is always a perception of creation or origin. To extend the argument in a more elaborate metaphysical fashion, creation or physical existence is the basis of all perceptions, but reality is ever present, even without perception or a human being who is capable of accounting or understanding. Therefore, creation and reality don't necessarily demand perception for their existence, but because matter and spirit are one with preexistence, knowledge, wisdom, accounting, or perception are inherent or unavoidable, integral parts of existence. The expression *reality= origin/perception* is not just an ordinary opinion but a dynamic declaration of the very nature of the enigma of the origin of physical created existence. The symbolic representation *r=o/p* actually recognizes that all transformations of energy are, in fact, mandatory by purpose of which is most probably with the anticipation of sin. The primary supporting argument, according to this theory of Christism, is that before God created the physical universal phenomena, there wasn't any evidence of constant or required energy transformation, and all energy interactions were without virtual energy loss. An analogy to this is the interaction of homogenous gas–in a container–which sustains no energy loss according to scientific experiments.

It must be fully understood that even the fact of creation is a spirit of perception of innovation. Because energy and the spirit of God has preexistence, the act of God's creation is but an act of transformations of themselves. Likewise, all perceptions of human knowledge are all perceptions of accounting or acknowledgement and innovation of what is created by God. This justifies those perceptions is never a permanent reality but an innovation (mercantile value) of reality, regardless that reality is perception because the spirit of God preexisted before the creation of the physical universe. Because of the preexisting union of energy (or the rudimentary forms of matter) and the spirit of God, the act of creation is an actual act of mechanielectrochemical process. And upon this fact the inquiry as to the mystical claim of God's act of creation is posted as the Jewish or Christian theory, e.g. "let there be light and there was light." Both religion and scientific concepts or theories of creation are not only completely diametrical, but they also both have apparent enigma relative to the nearest affiliation of the demand of absolute truth of reason and wisdom.

The philosophical relativism of the argument or opinion of the equation *reality* = *creation/perception, r-c/p*, has a very profound significance of the very nature of all universal existence. This opinion expresses the relationship that transformations of energy either by human innovations or God's creation are at the bounds of the second law of thermodynamics of heat/energy transfer and that all molecular aggregates or compounds are predisposed to disintegration because all energy given into a system is the same energy that will be given off by the system in due time, regardless of what form of energy. However, the equation $r = c/p$ does imply that perception (preceptor or beholder, except the gods) is mortal, regardless that reality and creation are immortal.

The black hole theory is a disaster theoretically, and it has very little relevance to any purpose, especially to the fact that if there is an origin or energy, therefore, it must not have any end. The equation $E = mc^2$ offered by science is only quantitative analysis of energy, but not in any insinuation provides any explanations of the origin of energy or the rudimentary forms of matter. Logically or philosophically a recycling Big Bang (and/or energy-consuming black hole) is stupidity. Man's greatest knowledge is just a joke when compared with the wisdom of God. The equation $r = c/p$ demands absolute immortality in all of its parts. Someday, somehow perception will eventually become a permanent reality. Presently, all perceptions and innovations are temporary in nature as reality, because nothing is immortal except the gods. Evidently, by all means of philosophical or logical proposition, because matter is a purpose and wisdom are inherent, the ultimate cause and value or motive of all reason and knowledge is a future event of immortality–and not of the spirit alone but of the flesh also. Therefore, the ultimate goal of perception is immortality, because anything else is of no value, and when immortality is realized, perception would be completely homogenized and thus bridle the emergence of sin. Therefore, the opinion $r = c/p$ denotes that the actual finality of creation is to be finished. At the present dispensation, immortality is contingent upon the demand of righteousness as defined in the structure of morality. However, the act of which immortality would be imparted is completely at the full discretion of the Deity but would be executed by God the Son (as the savior, Jesus Christ in religion).

The proposition of the equation $r = c/p$ should be completely understood for the purpose of understanding salvation or immortality. To provide an illustration on this relativistic principle ($r = c/p$) for an easy understanding is to consider this argument: suppose there are four locations or points called A, B, C, and D, and these locations or points are each occupied by diverse removable energy or matter. Naturally, points and between points are space and time while energy or matter (atoms) are creation. The presence of space and time between points provides hold and mobility of the energy or matter to be moved from one point to another upon demand. When one aspect of energy/matter at one location point is moved and interchanged from one location or point to another upon/by the demand of a preceptor, the new formation of locations and points therefore, is the new reality according to say preceptor X. Preceptor Y could also reshuffle or rearrange the place of energy or matter from one location or point to another distinct from the formation made by preceptor X. This illustrates how the creator allowed creatures to effectuate (although with only one general purpose of existence) various liberty of existence, including countless genetic modalities or configurations. (For further discussion see the Truth and Mathematics.)

To issue more relevance to the full understanding of perception, perception is an integral function of the accounting or pictorial/visual, sensual, mathematical or numeric, and philosophical/logical or thought processes. This analysis illustrates that, regardless, that thought process and its expression are very limited with the use of language/vocabulary or diction or any use of words; perception is not. And in logical inference, perhaps higher intelligence or the gods use just sensual, visual, or pictorial accounting of perception by or with the use of energy levels/gradations and sensations. Even scientists demand visual evidence to arrive at conclusions because mathematical figures alone never could account for the absolute truth.

The Unified vs. Separatist Theory of the Nature of God or Existence

All forms of religion that practice of formal religious ceremonial worship a definite or specific object regarded as God are separatist in their concept that God is an individual entity aside from a universal existence; e.g. the Christians who worship a personal God called Jehovah or Christ; the Muslim or Islam worship Allah, or at least his teachings, which is also very similar to Buddhism, on which religious practices are centered in philosophical teachings or creeds or beliefs which are derivative of the fact of reality of the presence or evil or death. Whether Christianity or Buddhism, the basic principles are identical in pursuit. The other forms of religion in the forms of cultures like those who worship fire or the sun or anything regarded as a divine being or creator also belong to the separatist understanding of the nature of God or existence.

The unified concept of the nature of God, though, is a concept that is not totally new in its overall scope, and it is much, much bigger than all practices of all religions combined. It is a system of thought that regards all knowledge, wisdom, philosophy, understanding, learning, ability, reckoning, accounting, recognition, acknowledgement, arithmetic, mathematics, and all mental processes of anything that possesses a mind or even the ability of anything like vegetation to grow or even the movement of all universal objects are all considered as operations with and of the spirit of God. Evil is regarded as an act or behavioral aberration or deviation form the natural/normal course of nature's structure of morality, and all other behaviors have their origin from the structure of morality that is placed by God in nature through the structure of the atom or matter.

There are two components of the nature of the spirit of God; the passive and the active. The passive spirit is imbued, for example, in human beings; it could be used either for good or evil, and, it is completely under the volition of the individual for its utility. This is what we originally called the freedom of choice. The active spirit of God solely belongs to God. It is used for the proper maintenance of the universal existence, and just one of these is the gravitational force. This active spirit of God is responsible for the mortality of the human being by way of and through the atom. This active spirit of God encompasses universal operations; it is also in direct relation to the very spirit of the universe which has the same operational characteristic with the human mind, though it remains distinct in its structure and has physical (molecular) properties. That man is made in the image (atomic and or subatomic particles) or God is a verity even from the Jewish scripture, from dust to dust.

The Purpose of God

In all wisdoms, whether they be of science, religion, or philosophy, there's only one possible objective as to which the meaning of the word God is meant/related to; existence. From here the ultimate definition of what is the purpose of God and his nature would be discussed in a unified fashion of both physical and philosophical manners. Because God the son has the burden of proof, he designed his universal existence in such a very magnificent cosmic structure. The intent of God to manifest himself or his being couldn't be more abundant and absolutely complete through the evidence of the presence of all colors. What other purpose of the existence of color except of the significance of presenting one's existence? And relevant to this purpose of God is the creation of living beings, one of which is the human being in the solar system.

God doesn't necessarily mandate that humans must recognize his existence in the form of all that is created, but the fact is, humans couldn't avoid such reality, regardless of whether man is given an absolute freedom of choice in such a way that he could manipulate matter/energy for the purpose even to the extent of a massive destruction of existence. But God is always amicably resilient to human follies: he couldn't be destroyed.

In the present reality of human existence, the sole purpose of God for man is to account for or enjoy the pleasures of universal/local existence. But such an intent became so complicated to achieve with the modern man that he has shifted his priorities. In fact, the Judaic Christian Scripture described in the book of Genesis that God had created man in the Garden of Eden, a notion which perfectly suggests the intent of God of the way in which man should live.

Since that accounting/reckoning/enjoying/beholding/acknowledging, etc., of existence could only find its essence with the power of choice, atomic and molecular mortality is indexed, and immortality became contingent, Although, it is not very clear in anthropology which one came first: death or sin, in the Jewish scripture sin came first and death is just the consequence. We don't necessarily have to unearth anything to start looking for the evidence because the chances of disappointment aren't worth the effort. In fact, the philosophical argument would do just fine so that even if we could find the answer as to why death came about, humanity would have available only two probabilities that he could deal with.

In this study, the path of emphasis deals with the fact that the possibility of death came first by nature because the creator anticipated sin; otherwise, if the principle of death is not incorporated in the original draft when the atom was first created, then God couldn't have the recourse when man committed his first transgression, thereby immortalizing all evils. Was God being stupid? Could He? No, absolutely not. God is absolutely just and practical and perfect in wisdom. Because this whole universal existence is one unified plan of creation, all operational modalities are universally identical. To verify this process physically, the amount of energy that has formed a tree trunk would be the same amount of energy used when it is burned, leaving a minimal residual energy in the ash, and all energy released is stored somewhere for recycling. Energy in equals energy out is a principle of thermodynamics. This same process of death and regeneration also applies to the death of a much, much bigger structure of energy (star/sun) in the universal space, regardless that a bigger structural decay death of a star may or may not support its ash structure and thereby disintegrate as theorized by the black hole proponents. But even if a black hole exist it has no major implication on the immortality of God the father. As has been previously discussed, the theory of the Big Bang or black hole couldn't possibly exist (read Truth and Mathematics), but even if they do, chances are God will remain immortal as has been previously discussed that the nothing (space and time) will preserve the universal physical existence as to the fact that no travel is possible in the absolute vacuum of empty space, relative to the fact of the physical definition of motion: that all motion or activity is either by the utility of push or pull of energy or both simultaneously, but since that absolute vacuum of space is completely void of mass, any intrusion of travel of motion into it is only relative to the distance a body is push by what x amount of energy.

The first and foremost member of the trinitarian nature of Deity is God the father as manifested by space and time, which has a responsibility to but is not limited to physical universal existence. First, he initiated the creation of the universe. Second, it holds and preserves the universe. Third, is supports all activities of all his creations. Without God the father (space and time) there's no creation; neither is there life of any form.

God the son is the second member of the Deity. And he was with God the father since the beginning of time. In fact, through the aid of God the father he transformed Himself into what we have as a physical universal existence. God the son created human beings, though not alone because in all existence the presence of God the father is needed. So, all physical realities are the creation of both God the son and God the father; otherwise, physical reality as we know it doesn't exist. Therefore, the whole universe mass is the embodiment of God the Son: we could call it Christ, even with respect to the Judaic Christian faith–in principle but not in physical embodiment.

The Holy Spirit as the third member of the Deity is very controversial in nature, because to account for his manifestation as a separate reality or entity is quite unexplainable; regardless, his presence is as prevalent and apparent with the reality of universal existence. Perhaps one of the functions of the Holy Spirit is to serve as the final hold or storage (postmortem) of all spirits of every living being. In other words, it will store and comfort–in waiting of the immortality of the flesh–the spirits of righteous human beings at the time of death. Although the Holy Spirit is by itself always a part of the universal energy from atomic to the universal mass, the Holy Spirit, therefore, participates in all creation activity but mostly on the molecular structure of energy; for example, in guiding the formations of DNA structures of both passive and active modulations.

Looking at the trinitarian nature of the Deity, it's actually a dynamic force with respect to the overall nature of creation as mechanielectrochemical process. This is the purpose of God: to create physical existence, not spiritual reality in that the human spirit is trapped in the flesh, and any act of salvation for immortality would be imparted to this same purpose. As already explained in this study, the nothing (God the father) and the physical universe (God the son) have created for themselves a law of conservation of energy which has been understood by human beings. Regardless of the fact that the black hole theory proposed a decay of energy as gray matter or what they have, and since that science still pronounced gray matter as matter, it therefore retains some residual energy with it; otherwise, science would have no option of detecting its presence. The opinion, therefore, of the black hole doesn't propose the mortality of the universe or energy even with scientific perspective. It would be impossible to assume the mortality of energy or matter or the universe, not unless the origin of energy itself is found and understood. Until such time or occasion will come, then and only then will we fully understand the nature of the proposition of whether there is no God. But as to the present dispensation, the presence of God is bearing affinity to the absolute truth, and science has full liberty of the option for the burden to disprove.

Reconciliation of Unified and Separatist Theory of God

Because God is righteous, he accepts all viable forms of worship, even to the extent of any modality, but notwithstanding the pure and honest intention. God considers all forms of worship as an expression of accounting or acknowledgment of his being. The reverse is also true, that all forms of accounting and acknowledgment of the care and understanding of nature might be acceptable as an act of worship; however, this form of worship is inseparable with its intent, and it's supposedly the ultimate duty of every human being with the capacity of intelligence or with the full awareness and understanding of existence. Salvation, therefore, relies on both what one does and in what one believes because the primary reason of intelligence is accounting with regard to faith to be regarded a preeminent regardless that faith and work will always be equal in value. One is inseparable from the other as God is inseparable from his spirit. Likewise with all existence if the spirit finds favor without the matter then there couldn't have been anything created taking into full account the idea that the spirit of God is preeminent of God the matter itself. When the Bible speaks of the son of God of Jesus Christ who has a physical existence, it is a verity (in terms of universal existence) in the whole stretch of philosophical argument and thereby in reality.

Religion perceives reality as unilateral to spiritual concepts as a diametrical to physics that reality is unilaterally a full physical matter, the domain of expedience belongs to perception and spiritual or philosophical wisdom and knowledge. Regardless, perception must allow and incorporate the accommodation of the understanding of natural laws that God himself created so that the end justifies the means and to stipulate that near absolute perception is required for the development of immortality of the spirit and the flesh.

It's therefore the calling or the advent of the theory of Christism to furnish such an adjunct perception of the nature of God or existence to bring to human consciousness of the third dimension of understanding of reality because God will only award salvation of immortality upon those who have taken a serious and sincere desire for the fulfillment or righteousness for the purpose that imparting immortality is a one-time irrevocable event. Therefore, the gods always exercise the option and preventive measure that defection would be impossible upon humanity's receipt of the gift of eternal life. The subject of the issuance of immortality is a deep and solemn venture demanding precise considerations on the part of the gods. If we human beings ponder nature and/or our existence, we could attend a complete understanding of why we are mortal. As the mortality of man is completely explainable, in fact, it's in the beginning available and contingent for humanity as the result of the transgression of the structure of morality, for without the availability or knowledge for mortality, man couldn't have known or accepted his creator or God.

Side Issue: Love and Marriage

Any theory presented must be tested upon its dynamics. The unified theory of existence does put itself into this test of social and interpersonal relationships. A human being's experience is an example of the living entity that this whole universal existence has created which has a very complex nature compared to all the rest. The unified theory of existence is not a theory that is created only to be made for mere empty idealism, but it has been in existence by physical and philosophical arguments and evidence, and its enlightenment is issued for its accounting or acknowledgment for its full utility.

One of the most basic and greatest needs of humanity is love and marriage, for the purpose of self-preservation. Humanity didn't create love and marriage. It's an inherent activity of nature (in the structure of morality) placed by our creator. In fact, it is also an act completely practiced by the lower forms of creation. And for simplification purposes, the word *Christism* must continue to be substituted/assumed in place for the unified theory of existence.

Although love and marriage have long been an activity of human beings, the practice has deteriorated, and more often than not, its deterioration has mostly benefitted professional healing operators of its mercantile value because most human beings lack the knowledge of self-realization.

Love and marriage actually have only two major components: one is the physical, and the other is expectation. Physical means the overall appearance of the parties in consideration, while expectation means intellectualism and idealism, regardless that it should be discretionary in nature. The expectation component of love and marriage has been the most vulnerable part that has been tremendously adversely affected by the advancement of human knowledge. In the modern human society, expectation has played a major role in the formation of marital status; however, it is also the major causation of the breakdowns of marriages. It also shouldn't be fully discounted that some marriages could also lead to destruction by both of the components of love and marriage, and once divorce has been granted by either human statutes or by the voluntary separation of both parties, rarely is that dissolution of marriage reversible. In most cases, it's irreparable.

Before it would be attempted to find the source of the problem of love marriage, it should be noted that in Christism, it's only God the matter that granted our worship or devotion or accounting or acknowledgment because the spirit of the gods doesn't demand our worship for its existence. It must be understood that in all existence the spirit and the matter, although one and inseparable, are two separate entities which have their own natures with distinct personalities that have a pre-agreed union. This can be compared to a molecule of one atom of sodium and one atom of chlorine which is a combination of two distinct natures, bur holds one particular purpose as table salt, and the principle could even extend deeper into subatomic particles. The argument would remain the same for all of creation and is the act or all the trinity of God/Deity.

Marriage is not a devotion for/to idealism but rather the devotion for the material/physical existence. So is the universal existence that it is not intended for the devotion or worship for the spirit but of the accounting and acknowledgment of the son or God, the matter, because the spirit of God and God the father are both unseen and immortal regardless of anything. But God the matter (son) granted to our accounting of its existence regardless that our accounting doesn't issue or preempt at any degree God's immortality. So, if the principle or Christism is transferred into the situation of considerations or human marriages, life would be more organized and fulfilling.

If matter (body) is taken out of existence (or from marriage) then what is left is a spirit which has no physical existence and which we simply call "empty." So, the sole purpose of marriage is the devotion of the pleasure of the flesh for the benefit of existence and for the fulfillment of the first structure of morality. Expectation, therefore, is just a secondary factor, and it shouldn't be the primary concern of marriage; otherwise, it would be very vulnerable to the easy prey of destruction. However, it shouldn't be confused that expectation is not very relevant in material existence, but its priority must in all occasions be secondary and totally discretionary in nature. And as long as the emphasis of this union is in the exact order of the union of love and marriage, it would be realized that the secondary (expectation) could serve as a strong, vibrant, beneficial component of the structure of the marital status. Expectation, therefore, should always be derived from a natural course of the marriage arising or motivated by the perfect mutual desire of passion of the physical affinity of both parties. Expectation is a wide spectrum of human activity; it could be religion, lifestyles, habits, personal preferences, etc., but mostly expectations its nature is mostly limited to idealism and cultural–lifestyle–gratifications of individuals.

Marital problems mostly arise when one expectation becomes the sole overriding factor in the union. And when one party fails to meet the demand of the expectations of the other, on most occasions the destruction of marriage is inevitable, and in most cases very detrimental and leads to irretrievable destruction. Of course, expectation is an avoidable part of marriage; it's what responsibility is accounted for, but when the demand of responsibility exceeds one's ability and capability, then a complexity of problems arises. In most cases, when the problem finds no solution. it leads to the unilateral or bilateral total destruction.

Lovers should learn, before into a marriage, that the physical compatibility must be the primary concern, as the spirit of the universal existence granted all worship to God the son the matter, for the purpose that all is to remain in existence. To fulfill the demands of the flesh is quite easy simple- "my yoke is easy… and my burdens are light" (a text from the Bible) –but to fulfill all the demands of the spirit is limitless and improbable. So, if we reverse the creation of a relationship placing expectation up front, then love and marriage would be a very complicated task rather than a simple physical attraction between the opposite sexes and thereafter try to live within each other's viable expectations arising from mutual love.

The modem man/woman has acquired a very complex existence and has created for himself/herself propositions of absolute expectations or ideals that often lead to the destruction of the free will of humanity. But when the principle of Christism would be reintroduced or rediscovered, then love and marriage relationships would be less demanding but more fulfilling. However, all marriages must be taken as individual cases because of the complexity of varied situations. In all existence there are not the same or exact duplicates of experiences and circumstances, and there shall be no place for complete generalization, as God always deals/adjudges each individual case, regardless of the general rules because oftentimes even the general rules have exceptions, and the tremendous power of choice given to existence must be observed at all times giving way to the arguments of the relative and absolute truths.

The importance of intellectual compatibility between parties is greatly relevant to selecting a mate because the contrary is uninteresting and, in most cases, non-productive, but its bounds remain secondary. A perfect union, therefore, is the proposition of the best overall considerations of the two components of love and marriage in its only order, but it should be taken as a relative absolute truth attributed to understanding the best chance could offer because universal as well as local episodes and experiences didn't preclude the power of choice, but rather even had welcomed all the propositions of risk because it's also the righteousness of God the (son) matter.

Even if Christism is transferred into a whole lot of issues, the principle stands unscathed because its central and supreme thesis is the physical life itself and not mere idealism. Christism also cuts through the hearts of absolute and totalitarian governments and/or systems of economical, moral, or ethical managements of society, even to the minute details of everyday life. Christism also gives essence to compromise, charity, and forgiveness, etc. Regardless of the fact that they are attributes of spirits, the intent is for the benefit of the body and not the spirit; otherwise, its sole virtue recoils to mere exhibition of empty idealism.

It's therefore evident that the major considerations in marital status on or before the commitment should be for the benefit of the flesh and not the spirit. Also, companionship is not a property of the spirit but of the flesh, so that when the consideration of expectation overlaps giving adverse effects to the physical marital relationship, the union of marriage should be considered as having reached to a point of being irretrievably broken, and a call should be made annul the marriage by either party or both parties. Christism has, therefore, proven its relative absolute verity as applied to love and marriage. The human spirit must serve the flesh or material existence; anything else is an empty idealism no matter how much pseudo-intellectuals could make it so morally palatable. Otherwise. what is the purpose of material existence? Do we say that physical reality is but a whimsical chance or creation of the spirit? So that the act of monasticism and the practice of celibacy would find justification? But in this quest the answer is an absolute falsehood and denial of the absolute truth of physical life. In conclusion. all expectations must serve the flesh and not the reverse order. Like the spirit of man must serve the body, the spirit of the universe (God) serves the purpose of the physical universal existence.

Christology in the Unified Theory of Existence (Christism)

In Christianity, (according to the Christian Bible) Jesus Christ is the center of its consideration as the Messiah who is the incarnation of the word; "the Word was made flesh". This messianic act of God represented the overall hope and salvation of humanity. Christ had sacrificed himself by being crucified for humanity's justification from all sins: past, present, and future.

Even if the Jesus event didn't actually take place, its implication is admissible in Christism, As the Christ in Christian religion is the physical embodiment of God, so it is in Christism; the whole physical universal existence is the embodiment of the Son of God (Christ). Similarly, the Christ in Christianity claimed the trinitarian deity of all the Gods: the Father, Son, and Holy Spirit as Jesus is the representative of the holy union for the of humanity. This concept is equally a verity (in Christism) outside religious faith. Perhaps it's a coincidence, or couldn't it be? Or perhaps these two concepts are a happenstance of the ultimate philosophical understanding of the reality disregarding the infinitesimal on the matter relating to the ideological, ethical, cultural, and other minor differences bur exalting their major emphasis and premise. If there will be a defeat of religion, it is of its strict and draconian observance of minor aspects of human life while Christism is majoring in major things.

The central message of the Jesus Christ event in religion is the redemption for the transgressions of humanity. And this redemption is also the justification solely as the act of God so that humanity could receive such benefits through faith, and such as an act of faith which is not relative with any good works. So, justification for all transgressions is received as an unearned gift. A free gilt of salvation without preconditions to except to accept. This notion of salvation expresses the profound love of God. The believer who receives justification understood and realized transgressions thereby committed a reciprocity of good works by way of the established moral/ceremonial laws (of the church) believed to be ordained by God. Technically, the concept of righteousness by faith has more binding significance or purpose to the ultimate rationality of religious economy and truth than the rationale of righteousness by work.

Whether or not there was a Jesus Christ of the Judeo-Christian religion, the spirit or idea of salvation for immortality has been instituted. Such philosophy of salvation was conceived during the era of human history when major scientific knowledge was virtually not in existence. This fact issues relevance to the idea that survival of life depends not only upon the necessity of the immediate demands of the flesh but also for the purpose of the preservation of all God's creation toward immortality. The structure of morality, therefore, was available even at the very beginning of human history.

The study of Christism provides the idea that human nature with its given structure of its anatomy and physiology is sustainable of immortality. The human physique couldn't have been the result of a transgression of moral and/or ceremonial precepts—that there was a physical transformation that took place after the fall of Adam and Eve— but rather was built and designed by God. Humanity's mortality is the result of pathogens, diseases, and the aging process, and such occurrences and events are not solely completely relative to moral transgressions alone. It must be in conjunction(s) with the intricate process of selection of who will not be mortal, as all records of the human major philosophy would be adjudged. Human mortality, therefore, must be understood as a temporary engagement of existence for the purpose of the immortality event to come. The sacrifice of the Christ in Christian understanding exhibits a relatively excellent philosophy of the relationship of salvation and death—relegated to the analogy of the condition of sleep. Also, in Christism as in religion, the work of salvation or immortality would be solely an act of the Son of God.

"I am Alpha and Omega... " serves as a biblical declaration of the intent of the authority of God. This also enunciates the plan of salvation. The word *Alpha* is self-explanatory, but the **Omega** might be contingent on some speculation that there might be an insinuation of the actual physical end of existence or energy. Even in scientific thought exists an ambivalence of the finality of the fate of energy, on the speculation of an ever-expanding universe, and at the same time issuing the notion of a black hole consuming energies into eternal oblivion. In Christian faith, as well as in Christism, Jesus Christ is the promise of eternity in scientific hypothesis the existence of a black hole is only a basis for the purpose of justification of the Big Bang theory.

Even if there exists a religious conspiracy of the existence of Jesus Christ or the whole Judeo-Christian faith, there's enough evidence presented by archaeologists that the worship of a Divine being existed long enough before the modern world. It should be pointed out that it's not only the Judeo-Christian religion that has an ancient concept of God. Some culture actually worships the volcano, sun, and etc., as a Divine being. As in any form of religious faith, the principle is so obvious that the spirit of God was and is in a form of communication. Honest mysticism or any exercise of a belier system of God must abandon arrogance for the fact that the absolute truth is only available through faith; faith, in the same token, is a matter of perception of the revelation of wisdom.

Philosophically, as well as of a symbolical inference, the Christ event of the Judeo-Christian faith is so far, the most refined form of expression of the sprit of the divine communication in religious forms. Even if the whole material and actual historical events of all of Christendom didn't take place, the evidence might just be quite relevant that the spirit of God moved and asserted its influence of communication, perhaps through the hardship and struggle of individuals and also with their victory and celebrations of happy and prosperous times. As it was mandated and self-evident that the knowledge about God is not now or never was confined or limited to just one culture or race but rather existed almost in a worldwide proportion, it was, therefore, when the whole world was completely innocent and pristine from the influence of scientific knowledge that the spirit of God was predominant throughout the planet Earth. Moreover, the message of the event of Christ in Christian faith exhibits parallel indications of philosophical as well some scientific truths.

Spiritualism vs. Christism

The fundamental concept in all the practice of spiritualism is based on the understanding of the fact of the ability of the human spirit to deny the needs of the body/flesh, because the flesh couldn't provide all of its needs and demands—aside from the bodily organs' functions, which are controlled by the active spirit of God—by the spirit; for example, the need for sex is initiated by the flesh but acquired by the spirit. Anything that the body needs outside of it is completely under the administration of the spirit of which the body itself is the medium and receiver/beneficiary of the actions. In other words, the theory in Christism that the spirit must serve the body in an absolute verity, but the service of the spirit must find its bounds with the structure of morality—a structure of morality based on physical and not on pure spiritual idealism.

The biggest mystery in all existence remains the question of immortality, and all other aspects of human experiences revolve around this single issue. It seems that the path of perception taken by the proponents of spiritualism is that the spirit of a human doesn't actually die with the death of the flesh, although this notion doesn't necessarily have any merit in reason or logic of the purposive process of creation, but that the practice of spiritualism has been repudiated not only by science but also within ancient history (it even existed in biblical times) that the continual use of the practice itself can't issue results of its claim(s), so to expound, it must remain as an empty idealism or pursuit.

However, nobody could ever deny the existence of spirits, but it's being is the function of a purpose not of itself but for the benefit of physical existence, because reality is perception. Any existence, therefore, has a knowledge or a purpose. The whole universe is a physical existence of God, particularly the Son of God, so it is a human being possesses a spirit. Unfortunately, some human beings understood themselves as having extrasensory perceptions; the sixth sense, psychokinesis, mental telepathy, and so forth. But time has proven these claims couldn't deliver concrete and substantive evidence.

The great fallacy of the nature and misconception of experiences of human spirituality is the general misapplication or misnomer of the term/word *spiritual experience*. The misunderstanding lies on the fact that the human spirit has the virtual capability/capacity to deny a whole lot of the demands of the flesh; one example is eating, drinking, love, etc. And even the proposition of its separate existence aside from physical realities like transcendental meditation and the use and utility of dreams been strictly misconstrued as a pure spiritual experience.

Human beings have been widely deceived regarding their understanding of one of the most precious gifts of existence: the gift of the spirit of the universe. Because of its very passive endowment, it has been largely misused if not completely misunderstood. This misunderstanding of the nature and use of the spirit is perhaps the greatest deception of all times, which even some of the greatest ancient philosophers have not recognized; thereby, its misuse has proliferated and been deeply established in human ordinary consciousness and assumed experiences.

The active and passive spirits in all created beings are all acquired at conception at the same time—the formation of these two entities gives way to a unique, particular, peculiar individual mind or intelligence. Their development synchronizes interdependently and inseparably from one another, and although they follow the structure of heredity and environmental factors/conditions and influences, the capability of spirit is never limited within these boundaries; regardless, the operational mechanism remains at the mercy of the physical realities or existence by which most philosophers have understood that the body is sinful. But it's the spirit that has been corrupted with its relationship of the supply and demand of the union. The corruption has to be attributed to what has been the deviation that occurred from the structure of morality and has further developed an enigma of religion, now a flesh and spirit separatism concept of human nature and the universe as a whole. And as this concept remains accepted and embraced, a whole lot or humanity would never be ready to accept the immortality of the flesh or matter in general. To believe that immortality is only to be imparted for the spirit is a denial of the purpose of the creator for creation. It is only God the father that is to remain in the special prerogative of spiritual immortality. The human spirit could only be temporarily stored (without the necessity of spiritual consciousness) in the bosom of God at the time of death.

A fact or existence is that the human spirit couldn't possibly exist outside the flesh. All its purpose is in the bounds and benefit of the flesh: otherwise no matter could have been created or creation is only by random chance by unknown cause and all wisdom remains to be wasted. To attempt, therefore to undergo or experience the separation of matter and spirit will fail because our thoughts and emotions will always have a material component. Also, this will defy any meaning of salvation or any act thereof, and immortality will have no derivative of wisdom and righteousness thereby also exhibit that God's act of creation is lacking solemnity and is but a mere whimsical experiment from an actual emotional perspective: the act of love or its antithesis, hate, always has a material objective—mainly physical existence. In actual physical reality, the enormous inherent mechanism of human physiology of is capacity and capability against diseases as an attempt to preserve physical existence is an intelligence or mechanism—provided even in the creation of the atom by our creator; otherwise it could have been unnecessary if there is a possibility of immortal spirit as the ultimate projection or anticipated fate of creations.

All created organisms, therefore, are deprived of real, conceivable, pure spiritual experience, but it's only presumed or presupposed due to the presence of the spirit, especially in human beings. The act of faith has been misconstrued as a spiritual experience primarily because its purpose is for a truly spiritual God the father who exists only in spirit, but the object of faith could not suppose the means of existence and that the unseen creator has no demand but that worship should be directed to his begotten son who has a physical existence and whose physical reality also imparted into all matter a sole administrator of all physically verifiable activities of creation. The indisputable unified theory of the union of matter and spirit is the fact that a truth is a derivative of both philosophical wisdom and coherence and physical examination and evidence. To dispute this theory would be relegated to separatism. One classical extreme example of this is the Jim Jones syndrome: a very bold undertaking of self-murder due to the lack of philosophical understanding of the real nature of creation and the purpose or creator thereof.

To understand fully the ultimate disposal of the human spirit upon the demise of the flesh is to correlate cognition with the nature of the very basic elements or constituents of human bodily existence. As it is self-explanatory that the nature of the anatomy and physiology (and all other human organs) or human structure is nothing but for the execution of the acquisition for the sustenance of the needs of the most basic element of physical human existence, which is the somatic cell. The life process continues within the cell itself for the production or replication of the DNA which is itself nothing but a complex structure or formation of a few atomic elements. Any inquiry of purpose (creation) must therefore be directed to the enigma of why various energy structures of atoms do exist. Do fortuitous events have any relevance as to why hydrogen, carbon, nitrogen, oxygen, and other necessary atoms/elements existed for the formation of life? Or did the existence of these elements originate by a purpose? Universal existence, as well as life on planet Earth as we know it, has only two probabilities of its origin: either by chance (Big Bang) or purpose (God). The formation of amino acids as the building blocks of life could either be understood to have come about by chance or directed by a purpose of creation.

If all physical existence is the product of the works of a creator/ God, then the spirit and wisdom of such a creating force must also have his residence and/or direct influence in/with the most rudimentary energy structure of the atom. The evidence to support this philosophical argument is itself within human nature of the presence of two spirits in every person: the active and the passive. The materialism school of thought hypothesized that all the mind activities are based on physical properties. Rene Descartes believed that God and mind belong to one reality and the matter or body to another. Uniting these two concepts together explains the true reality of man as having a trinitarian nature, and in a quite similar fashion the universal physical existence as a whole has a trinitarian nature. Fortunately, some Christian religious concepts enunciated a trinitarian nature of God.

The active spirit of man is the function of the matter/body, while his passive spirit is imparted by his creator for the mind. The passive spirit is also the conscious mind which is capable of denying most of the demands of the flesh regardless that its residence of existence is bound in the flesh; thereby a unity and agreement is the goal of conduct as the mode of righteousness for life; otherwise, robotic moralism or righteousness is to what relevance deemed but selfishness of power, where the consciousness of evil is available and perpetuated

The imparted passive spirit in man, which is also a part of the universal spirit of God, which became the conscious mind or spirit of man, is a reality of which man is not vested with actual physical or mental perception about it except the knowledge of assumption. In simple words, regardless of the fact that man could know that the spirit of God is in him, he has no actual feeling of consciousness of its presence, aside from some instances in which honest individuals could experience unexplained phenomena or events, perhaps as an attempt of the spirit of God as an intervention for ultimate necessity for sole personal purposes or for the general revelation of truth.

At the time of a person's demise. and because everything belongs to God, everything will return to God (from dust to dust [Genesis 3:19]) in a similar act of energy transformation. But how the passive spirit of God was utilized will be a record for the judgment day for the final disposal or eternal life.

Even in modern times. as in recent history, a huge number of people still were tied to the belief of the immortality of the soul. And this concept permeates to most existing major and minor religious organizations in both Protestantism and Catholicism. And the most extreme cultic groups actually commit suicides with the ambition to be one with God. But regardless of whether one has to commit suicide or not, the basic anomaly of the conviction of the immortality or the soul is very pervasive in human understanding and effectuates divergence of rudimentary lifestyles.

In the book of Genesis in the Christian bible, the concept of immortality has been taken into consideration and on one particular occasion, on the temptation of Eve by the serpent in the Garden of Eden ("...thou shall not surely die..."). This statement, regardless of its physical verity, a proposition of deception. But a much more logical inference could be deducted from the Garden of Eden event of the concept of the origin of sin and mortality, it's self-evident that the spirit corrupted the flesh; it's the spirit or mind that committed the transgression. not the flesh or body. Likewise, the judgment upon which immortality would be issued should be a consideration on the spirit or mind.

Any speculation bearing insinuation of any immortality of the spirit or the flesh before the judgment day is in denial of the concept of the act of sin itself. Sin and immortality couldn't coexist; otherwise, mortality has no purpose, and sin would never have any retribution. At the demise of the flesh, the spirit of man returns to God without consciousness but a record of how the privilege of life was used.

The Faith

Since the nature of creation is unified, to understand human nature must be related to its affinity to the nature and purpose of his creator. The validity of all speculations on human nature must therefore be intrinsic to the most honest speculative understanding of the nature of the whole universal existence in terms of possibility and its prospect of the pursuit of absolute truth regardless that the absolute truth is not limited to the perception of the physical reality. If it is so, then physical reality is bound to its own creation of mortality and immortality. Thereby, it's the ultimate search and pursuit of humanity; otherwise, human immortality is merely to be constrained to the progression of natural phenomena destined by his creator to be dispensed as directly proportional to how one used his God-given talents and abilities relative to all of nature and faith in his God.

Since it's not sustainable to believe that the universal mass/energy couldn't possibly be infinite, and its possible present existence in space could only be attributed and understood that the nothing has an inherent force, nor that any motion is possible without the presence of nothing (space) within and without of any given mass or energy, it's therefore conclusive that only the continual interaction of nothing and something has created intelligence which must be present both in organic and inorganic entities because all living forms are derivative of the atomic structure.

Ultimately, the "which came first" inquiry must be answered. The fact that the universal mass/energy couldn't exist without the nothing (space), it's therefore an imperative deduction that nothing (space/void) preexisted before anything. And of the fact of the existence of a purpose in all various atomic or subatomic energy structures, there was then a preexistence of knowledge that was responsible in the formation of the matter. The mystery of how the nothing created something is not possible to have a solution for understanding because in itself the nothing is infinite of its nature and size, and who could possibly understand infinity, and if infinity could be understood then it's finite. And if there's no infinity there couldn't have been a physical existence.

In the present era of the dispensation of the knowledge of physical sciences, momentous achievements have been very surprising, and there is the possibility that all existing physical realities could be understood through inventions and innovations of technological advancements. It seems that humanity has an explanation and solution to anything that is. It's therefore a presumption of understanding that anything that could be seen and have a physical mass is within the realm of human perception, which is a translation of the capability of an energy structure to understand its structure within and without of its organism—from a single cell to the highest variation, i.e., humanity, although humanity has yet to understand or believe the knowledge and wisdom of its ancestors: the atom and/or beyond the atom which is God the father (the nothing). It remains foolish in the realm of physical sciences to think that there's a knowledge and wisdom inherent in space or nothing itself. But to blame humanity for its inability to understand the wisdom of God (nothing, space) is to deny the fact that the nothing/void couldn't be understood nor that any organism whose existence is based on an energy structure would ever be able to see or understand the very nature, or what constitutes the nature, of God the father—the nothing—for the very reason that the nature of the nothing is energy without structure, regardless that is has a nature that is unseen and unpalpable.

It's an obvious reality both philosophically and scientifically that no physical reality could exist without the nothing for it's impossible that this whole universe must be filled up with an infinite mass—solid or liquid, forget gas— at the very beginning of time. It's more philosophically realistic to attribute the beginning of the universe from the standpoint of the nothing rather than that an energy could have preexisted without the nothing at the same time or beforehand. Likewise, it's more philosophically imperative that the absolute truth could not alone be a product of research and breakthroughs of physical scientific knowledge for the final reason that the origin of energy couldn't be found (beyond the meaning of motion/force: potential or kinetic). In fact, it should be the reverse order, that it's only with the honest seekers of truth that a final philosophical understanding of the nature of the universe could participate in the final days of dispensation of the final truth, and it would only come through faith.

It's only, therefore, through faith that we are able to relate to the spirit or wisdom of God regardless that it is an unseen nonphysical and interaction is with all physical realities or beings because the magnitude of is presence is within and without the whole universal phenomena. In humanity, faith is the expression of the unity of physical matter and spirit in terms of the spirituality of humanity. This union creates every distinct individual through the modalities and variations of environmental and hereditary factors. Any individual who limits his understanding to physical realities alone and/or relegates physical reality to subordinated status or attention lacks true faith in his creator. And for the virtue that God is just and holy, humanity is given the freedom of choice.

It is not because man is made or created in the image of God the son (the universe) or in the likeness of the union of the spirit of God and matter that is inherently vested of immortality, nor is the human

51

lack of inherent possession of immortality an inherent evidence that he couldn't be awarded immortality, nor that the human could have an understanding of the righteousness of God, regardless of the capability to commit transgression is irrelevant in that sin or evil is preconceived by God. The fact that humans don't have immortality is the predisposition that they will have; otherwise, how could man have the ability to recognize it? Thereby a precondition for immortality is inherent, and that is faith. Because immortality would be bestowed with the precondition of the knowledge of it, it therefore couldn't be inherent by any means: it's therefore a verity that all wisdom is inherent for a purpose with the virtue that all creation itself is a purpose.

The fact that the universal creation is created by a purpose is the evidence to support the argument that God the son/universe is immortal; otherwise, logic or reason is not available, nor a physical reality was made, therefore it sufficeth to say that purpose and matter are one. And this purpose is evident even in the theory of evolution, regardless that its proponents disagree, but their disapproval doesn't have any impact on the extensive direction nor did any general insinuation have influences in the final human destiny, regardless that human thoughts and actions have a major role with individual immortal salvation. Evolutionist practitioners had missed, if not completely disregarded, the role and direction or participation of an intelligent being in the progressive evolutionary process—if ever evolution really did occur. Though it's philosophically admissible, it's not an absolute mechanism of truth. The assumed random act of a cell mutation couldn't possibly have happened in a very logical pattern if nature alone directed its own evolutionary act of all the species. Even the notion that life on Earth might have originated from somewhere doesn't contradict or void the notion that creation is a deliberate act of a creator, for the presence of life alone is enough truth to justify a purpose or the presence of deity regardless that one may have enough arrogance to be deceived of oneself of self-creation.

Perhaps the most fundamental contribution of Buddhism to humanity is the exposition that the spirit of man is not a function of the body alone, and such spirit, regardless that it's an integral part of the mind, remains the mystery of creation of every uniqueness of every individual respecting the random act of the freedom of procreation. It's, in fact, the power that is responsible for allowing the capacity and capability of the mind to either obey or disobey all the prompting (needs in priority) of the body. If the mind is operating alone, then it must be completely under the command of the flesh so that man is a robot. The spirit of creation in every individual is completely unknown or concealed from our senses or knowledge. However, every individual could relate to the spirit of God only through faith primarily because we could never see God aside from the universal creation as the only physical manifestation of the creator. So that the biblical expression that we are the sons and daughters of God is philosophically veritable.

In order for an individual to possess a firm foundation of faith in his creator, it's imperative that such a rational individual must have a good realization or information of conflicting issues affecting the overall existence of its nature, including universal phenomena, for the fact that true faith is not just a word belief system but a dynamic force, regardless that it's based on a system of belief itself. In a very simple analysis, wisdom is not limited to the vestal just for an ordinary survival mechanism, but rather it links anyone to a very simple act of faith. Faith is simple, and to understand the requirements of faith is even more simple, for nobody is obligated to understand the infinite nature of God, which is not intended to be understood completely but rather only to be accepted. And this acceptance is the major basis of a dynamic faith. The secondary requirement of faith is its object. And the primary basis of faith simply acceptance, the nature of the object of faith likewise simple. Faith is a word with a broad spectrum of use that constitutes or has an affinity with the act of worship and piety. God the creator intended (but never demanded) the object of worship and faith to be a thing that's seen like the physical existence. In simple terms, the object of faith is the respect for all life and the universal physical nature of existence.

Let us extend this principle in a clearer manner with the logic of cause and effect. The cause of faith is the acceptance and acknowledgment of the unseen nature or our creator (the nothing), and the effect of faith is to serve that God. To serve that God is to serve our self, fellow man, and nature. If there's no realization of the existence of God, then faith doesn't exist. And since our creator doesn't need material things from us for his existence, the only way we could serve God is to respect what he had created in the greatest commandment: "love thy neighbor as thyself." Now that the basis and object of faith is fully understood, one big question must be answered to level out all doubts regarding the presence of mortality, pathogens, and evil behavior.

All life activities and behaviors are motivated and inspired. Even the worship of monks or priests in seclusion or in the midst of mass or society are inspired and motivated. The amount and nature of the inspiration and motivation is what determines the nature of the goal or priority of action. An individual inspired and motivated by a love For God could become a devout follower of a religion or a cult; an individual may be inspired by a lover could conceive a very admirable poem or a song. And the case goes on with all the rest of life's activities of all life forms. Even God might have had an inspiration and motivation when he created the whole universal existence. This inspiration/motivation and priority/goal relationship is analogous with the logic of cause and effect.

A balanced amount of cause and effect or inspiration and priority must be sustained for an organism to maintain a normal life or action. This balance is called *moral objectivity*. When an imbalance occurs between the amount of inspiration and priority, a situation arises which brings about a detrimental effect on behavior. Take, for instance when the impulse of self-preservation becomes the only predominant force in an organism. Most if not all of the other parts of the structure of morality would be jeopardized, and the result is an extreme selfishness and greed.

The natural direction of inspiration or motivation will always tend to move upward to become, if possible. the dominant force in one's activity. On the other hand, a goal or priority tends to find motivation and inspiration to fuel/energize its operation. The right amount or combination of these two forces creates a well-balanced or stable nature of the life of an organism.

Whether or not there's substantial evidence of physiological and/ or pathological origins of the nature of the imbalance for the ruin or the misuse of either one or all of the constituencies of the structure of morality, there's no clear understanding of why and how pathogens themselves came about, because to question their origin is inherently the same dilemma as asking the question of the origin of all other organisms. The question of mortality is to answer the philosophical origins of transgression on the basis that creation or matter has a purpose. So, what is transgressed is the answer to what is morality or what was right that went wrong.

If transgression resulted in a material or physical punishment or retribution, it suggests, therefore, that the nature or the object of the morality or righteousness that was transgressed must be material or physical. It must be taken into consideration that the purpose of creation is physical existence: therefore, the object of all statutes or decrees issued by the creator must be primarily for the preservation of physical existence. It's illogical to assume that human beings possessed an immortal spirit and that it's subject to physical or spiritual laws, and. if all the act of creation is finished, that the spirit of man is immortal. If the preceding situation is true, that human has an immortal spirit inherently given by God at the time of creation, then what is the purpose of wisdom, enlightenment, law, and order, the impetus for the best coherence of thoughts and the pursuit of knowledge and understanding? If man has an immortal spirit, then all activities of an organism should be very limited to just barely surviving without regard to good and evil. But the reality is it does not. Some humans, though not all, achieve and pursue wisdom and understanding and even seek the very origin of all existence. Some human beings who don't believe in the existence of a creator (who had given us purpose) but continue to try to answer the question of the origin of existence to acquire immortality are quite stupid.

Immortality is itself the ultimate purpose of a universal existence. And if immortality is only given for the spirit and that spirit is existing within flesh which is mortal, why live in the flesh? There is, therefore, a purpose in the flesh, isn't there? In fact, there are more purposes given in the flesh than in the spirit regardless that it bears the dilemma of mortality.

Mortality, therefore, is a transgression of a purpose. And that purpose is physical existence with an operating principle as the structure of morality which could sustain immortal life in the flesh despite pathogens and without the retrograde effect of the aging process.

Immortality became an issue of salvation. At this point of the study, the argument of the evidence presented is both physical and philosophical in nature; the existence of a creator becomes indisputable, or at the very least becomes with the best of probability. After all, what could physical sciences offer us of our chances of immortality, but a theory of a general relativity which also had faulty arguments regardless of its mathematical grandeur? Even in the case of the theory of general relativity, it failed to provide the very origin of the matter that been calculated, and it declared itself as the origin of all things, otherwise, physical science couldn't proceed but would wait for religion for vindication.

Pure philosophical arguments like mathematical verity couldn't bring about immortality, but rather immortality will lend itself for use, and it seems it needs some proposition of righteousness by faith. But regardless of how much purity and virtuous actions could be presented to amend a broken trust (structure of morality), some act of salvation on the part of God is required, primarily for the very reason that the principles of natural laws that have been originally encoded and acquired (during the process of a sinful life behavior) in the DNA which governs the mechanism of the perpetuation of self-preservation. And because the creation process is universally unified, what happens on Earth will happen in heaven or what happened in heaven will happen on Earth, meaning that when man suffered God suffered. The plan of creation must have an anticipation of the coming of sin, with the accommodation of contingency.

The Plan of Salvation

Science posted and entertained the idea of an ever-expanding universe. This theory illustrates the ambiguity of the principle of the Big Bang or black hole. This concept of a black hole violates the law of motion or the first law of thermodynamics. An ever-expanding universe is a proposition of an infinite universal mass/energy. To extract rationality from the study of physics to consider the nature of a pure spiritual reality is an obscurity and as misleading as the theory of general relativity (as a theory of origin) whose consideration of time and space is limited between points that were created from a Big Bang event (alleged) which happened sometime at the beginning of time. Also, an ever-expanding universe couldn't blindly be acknowledged to mean immortality for humanity, because the consideration of the black hole is not reconciled.

Physics and the related sciences obviously couldn't provide all the answers of the enigma of local and universal existence; therefore, it should be treated as just another perception of creation for the temporary reality humanity is presently in. It's up to the individual's personal choice and discretion to direct his/her own destiny based upon personal perceptions of all available knowledge that has been brought for consideration. This is what should be predominant and shouldn't be abrogated or restricted of use and access or minimized in any manner. To try to understand immortality or salvation (which is yet to be in their full facets) is to understand human mortality (which a present their full facets) is to understand human mortality (which is a present reality in all respects). This proposition's (immortality) pursuit must take into full account the

57

very nature of human physical anatomy and physiology. Analysis should be taken into consideration of whether the present human anatomy and physiology will be sustained during the immortality state, or shall it be changed or revised? For the purpose of analysis, we need to go back to the knowledge of perception to understand for what purpose human anatomy and physiology originated. Although it's very obvious that human structure is but a survival mechanism, it must be also understood that immortality is the ultimate preservation of physical life or existence. It must not be forgotten that the theory of general relativity equation has some use—that energy is matter and matter is energy, and it should be or must be a reversible equation. Regardless, some had extended the theory with irreversibility, to put forth a "big crunch" proposition. Will there be a full spiritual reality or a recycling of matter if the theory is correct? Even the Big Bang theory is not at all an empty proposition. And even if the matter and energy equation is reversible, it's not the full rational basis of immortality but the ultimate cause of temporary mortality of which present human experience is based upon the perception of our creator of the anticipation of sin. So that if the "big crunch" recycles, it eliminates the sinful individual who acquired the atomic/subatomic particles.

Mortality therefore might be conceived as a perception of God which has several elements:

1. Anticipation/retribution of sin
2. Knowledge of God (to accept or not to accept that there's God); also the knowledge of good and evil and absolute freedom
3. Instruction for immortality

Perhaps the intrinsic value of the theory of the black hole and the Big Bang is to serve as an extension of the idea that nobody by any means could escape the retribution (as a recourse) of God. And it doesn't necessarily have relevance with its merit in itself of its probability but as a viable recourse of instruction unless humanity thinks otherwise and hardens its heart (take into consideration that some human beings actually believe they become one of the stars in the heaven when they die). Also, this notion should serve as serious consideration that it's not at all stupid to admit that there's retribution by God.

It should be seriously considered that energy couldn't possibly exist from a cause or origin nobody could possibly understand and just will self-destruct into eternal oblivion (which even science couldn't explain how energy will forever end) as the Big Bang/black hole theorist wanted every human to believe. If science thinks that to believe in the existence of God is stupid, then how could science explain its stupidity of assigning an end of the energy of which they don't have a clue how it began or where it came from? And it must be well noted that science can only define energy mostly in terms its material particles in a form of potential and kinetic energies.

Because salvation and immortality require certain amounts of knowledge, although God might allow to the demand of rationality in some cases. any pursuit to understand this must in the realm of the elements of human perception in relation to what could be the perception of the creator or God's overall purpose of creation. As has been presented previously in this study. the ultimate purpose of God the father is for the creation of the physical universe which includes in it human beings. In other words, the deity (trinity) has transformed itself with the purpose of what we human being now perceive as ourselves and the whole universal physical reality.

Combining the structure of morality and the elements of mortality, a fundamental understanding of the purpose of God could be grasped: that human structure and mortal condition is but a transitional mechanism for understanding the last act of God's purpose which is immortality not only for the spirit but also for the flesh. The question whether or not human anatomy, physiology, and metabolism will be retained during immortality could only be given a pure speculative because the final act of God's creation couldn't possibly be fully anticipated by human intellect.

From the perspective that there's a creator therefore, the ultimate purpose is the creation of intelligent beings, such humans, which is also an act of evidence that the creator must possess intelligence. Because mortality is assumed as a perception of the creator not limited to the anticipation of anomaly or sin, such perception of a creator is the only evidence of all energy transformation or metabolism of fusion and fission or the nature of energy (subatomic or molecular) which is implemented universally. perception of mortality, therefore, is what determined human anatomy and physiology.

Human perception has its origin (in principle) with the perception of the creator. It would be impossible for human beings to distance or separate their perceptions from God, from which is the only reality of their (human) observations. Any intervention of salvation for immortality. therefore, must be solely the initiative of God contingent with human faith and righteousness, for which such righteousness must be derivative from the observance of the structure of morality and/or that when the condition had been met the demand for God to have a change of perception was amiable to human immortality.

However. the perception of science–especially of the possibility of a black hole and the "big crunch" –couldn't ascertain absolute truth about the nature of such observations of the nature of the immediate (to human) observable part of the universe. The only assumption of absolute truth is to come to realization that God must, in one way or another, want humans to understand the nature or possible future course of creation. Philosophically, the black hole or a Big Bang (crunch) is a theory awarded for the purpose to inculcate that the universe is unified and that the whole universal and local phenomena must undertake one action of change for the purpose of immortality so that humans don't assume responsibility or try to implement (though impossible) for himself the nature or condition of immortality so that every intelligent being in the universe must recognize the creator's act for immortality

Human reason demands coherence, so might also God; therefore, we must perceive that God demands or implements for himself coherence of his nature or his knowledge. Our relationship with God, therefore, with the issue of predictions or prophecy must stand coherent in philosophy, as well as the existing laws of nature, but with full respect to what's only available human wisdom. In this respect, God's and humanity's perceptions must in one way or the other have a reciprocity for one purpose toward the ultimate act of creation (immortality) relative to the learning process of life's mortality. As already evident in the unified structure of universal physical phenomena, this whole universe is acting under one gravitational force. It already been proposed (also in this study) that the universe must be alive and it's the embodiment of God (the son). All local or universal phenomena must be unified in purpose from its beginning to its full realization of eternity (the essence of the biblical expression: "I am the Alpha and the Omega"). The implications of whether there's a relevance of the realization of the notion on the actual occurrence of all universal events in regard to its benefits or detriments—or is not obvious or understandable, but as far as the logical inferences and/or objectives of religion and scientific knowledge are concerned, it seems that the notion or idea of a unified universal purpose is very evident. And if human perceptions knew all the results of every proposition of actions and events, then absolute freedom is not available or warranted of its objective.

It's therefore clear that mortality constitutes: freedom, sin, understanding/perception, morality, conscience, righteousness, learning/responsibility, appreciation, and selection/election for the coming immortality. These dimensions of human existence, regardless that it was preconceived by God to its full execution, are always at the full discretion of every individual. This is the justice and mercy of the creator. Without full freedom from the aspect of a creator, absolute justice is not possible, and without absolute justice God could only be perceived as a draconian and the act and/or purpose of creation would lack sincerity. All creation across the universe must therefore have undergone at some point a dimension of mortality (but not necessarily committed transgression). And because the process of creation didn't happen in a snap of time, the coming of immortality will follow the increment of time across the universe.

It must be fully understood that mortality is the only possible and viable dimension of reality upon which God and immortality could be accepted or rejected, and upon this basis love, faith, hope, etc., or their respective antitheses, are kept, understood, and exercised. Unfortunately, the majority of humanity seems to have fallen into the chasm of unilateral materialism, and on the other hand some had flirted with the concept of full spiritualism, even to the extent of denying the complex needs of the flesh. Although, morality is the demand of necessity (as might be God's point of view) and perhaps also the mother and causes of perceptions, it doesn't necessarily affect the commission of sin or transgression. Mortality in the most profound analysis is purposely a wait for immortality based on the argument that the present reality is just a perception (by a purpose) of the creator and humanity; for example, the concept of the black hole and "big crunch," regardless that they might just be fortuitous (conditional) events. The message is a message already awarded by a purpose/mortality and thereby must be a universal event that might not be avoided, notwithstanding sin or righteousness. This dimension (mortality) of perception by both the creator and his creations is but a temporary reality as expressed by the previously discussed philosophical equation $r=c/p$.

Immortality therefore is a part of the whole universal evolutionary process. And as the universal process of creation progresses into its culmination, all knowledge across the universe will incrementally advance toward the ultimate purpose of the creator. It's not, therefore, disagreeable to assume that some created beings somewhere in the universe might have already gained an immortal dimension of reality.

As the whole universal evolutionary process progresses, so does the intellectual condition of humanity increase. This is an indication that the universe is evolving toward immortality. But the knowledge of immortality is not a coercive force; it's to be chosen. It's a privilege to be accepted or rejected. It's the very reason God has given humanity an absolute freedom of choice of in what ways an individual will invest his/her talents and perceptions. As knowledge progresses, the criteria of judgment also must be relative to the current dispensation. Because there is no mechanism to stop universal time and space as it progresses into its full purpose, humanity is bound to the reality of God. Humanity must obey God, not the other way around, regardless that an absolute freedom of choice is always at the utility of every individual to accept or reject the current dispensation of wisdom.

Perhaps the greatest hurdle of change is with the philosophy of the unilateral practice of materialism, and it's unenlightened to believe that God will always want to save even those who don't believe in God or immortality. The concept of unilateral materialism is relevant for those who are willing to invest all their concepts of reality of the present life. The theory of materialism has been misunderstood by its proponents of its utility on the basis that they had applied the knowledge unilaterally or one-sidedly. Materialism must be a concept awarded for the purpose toward the understanding of the active spirit of God the son (matter). Diametrically, the passive spirit of God has also been misused and misunderstood by the proponents of spiritualism or those who believe in the immortality of the spirit or soul.

Materialism is a mandatory and necessary concept, but those who received the impartation didn't recognize that it should be a knowledge or wisdom that is to be exercised and utilized in conjunction with spiritualism. Likewise, the wisdom of spiritualism always has to be associated with materialism. Any lifestyle that is exercised aside from the union of materialism and spiritualism and which still expects the salvation of immortality is haphazard. But because the structure for salvation is in itself a concept or perception, the ultimate, sole author would be left alone to the creator because all actions, whether physical or spiritual, must be judged by their intent. And since that salvation must be a conditional concept, it's the very essence of human beings to be endowed with so much capacity and capability of varied perceptions. This is the purpose of Christism, a study that issued a third dimension/choice of perception of reality: a unified concept or theory of the trinitarian nature of human beings as well as the universe, and that the universe as a whole is but one universal purpose under the administration of a creator.

Materialism is a very credible concept, as far as its argument that all existence—even the spirit—has a physical element; therefore its proponents have miscalculated its purpose and intent even to the extent of denying any existence of a creator The study of Christism found a different situation because of the undeniable presence of the nothing/void that must have a force without any material reality, and without the nothing/void there's no possibility of the existence of any material or physical reality in the most profound analysis of philosophy or reason.

Nobody must be instructed by any means to deny the necessity of the concept of materialism for it's the only other part of all creation, but it must be embraced or understood with the existence of the creator which is the nothing. It's only in the union of the nothing (spirit) and something (matter/energy) that the whole universal physical phenomena could possibly exist and be capable of the process of thinking.

Salvation for immortality, therefore, could only be understood and appreciated if the evidence to support the existence of a creator is strong enough for the consideration of every individual perception. It's recognized that every action has a purpose, and every lifestyle is the direct result of an individual perception or understanding of reality. So, must salvation or immortality be awarded for the direct effect of every individual's perception and action. Even perception of faith is an action. So, in order to have a good concept of salvation, it's a must to understand one fundamental proposition of the structure of creation.

Perhaps the ultimate question to be answered regarding whether immortality is possible consider the need to understand the most basic structure of the most basic element of all universal structure of every physical created reality; heat: light as having mass and energy structure, and gravity, which doesn't have mass and energy structure but is a force. These explained phenomena are directly related to the motion or action and are accountable by their behavior or effects, unlike the nothing/void, which is a huge force yet has no mass, no energy structure, and couldn't be accounted by physical means or effects. So, by way of philosophical deduction, the trinitarian nature of existence remains: the matter and the two spirits (passive and active).

The most distinguished expression of materialism is the quest and exposition of the general relativity theory which seemed to have explained the nature of energy by way of material equivalents. Light and heat from the sun, for example, are explained by science as being the direct product of the atomic nuclear activity of fusion. Likewise and furthermore, the heart of the theory of materialism is the undeniable reality of metabolism, which has both universal principle and exists in all life forms. The energy (heat and light) from the sun is the only source of all life on planet Earth. Heat, its absorptions, and its releases are derived from motion. a motion as a direct result from either molecular or nuclear activities. The Big Bang and "big crunch" theorists extended the notion of the theory of $E=mc^2$ in the universal reality and scope. the Big Bang and the general relativity theories don't explain the nature of the origin of energy but explain that energy made matter the physical component of reality and the matter into energy.

If the smallest manifestation of energy is radiations, heat and light, which are derived from shift of motion or energy level structures, then energy is motion and motion is energy. The idea of a "prime mover" is, therefore, a philosophical analysis that must be embraced with the theory of materialism. The prime mover (creator) must have a force and a matter over which to exert or operate this force. By philosophical deductions, the prime mover is itself the object being operated because matter is energy and energy is motion and motion is energy: therefore, motion is also matter. The prime mover, therefore, is also life; it's also the whole universal physical and metaphysical phenomena and purpose and is a physical force that is completely alive with intelligence and wisdom or spirit. It's therefore like a human being (in the most basic sense) but in the form of a universal physical reality.

But does this prime mover or motion have a separate physical reality from the universal physical reality, or does the universe have an infinite mass, power, or energy? By reason or philosophical arguments, it is not probable; it's the essence of the theory or understanding or knowledge of materialism. It's the impartation of the wisdom of the spirit of God that the universe (the son of God) has a definite form and scope of reality: a finite universe(s). Regardless that the universe is finite in its mass and structure, human knowledge and/or instrumentations still has/have a limited understanding and observation. Although the human perception, according to the Big Bang and general relativity theorists, has a proposition of its understanding and material calculation of its overall mass it must only be a concept that the human holds as a temporary assumed reality.

Since science (materialism) and philosophy (spiritual) both concur on a finite universe, and the purpose of the prime mover must be the creation of a universal physical reality, the prime mover, therefore, is not alone. The law of motion requires space. The transformations and formations of energy levels or locations could only take place between points of space or energy structures, and motion couldn't avoid the element of time. Time and space aren't physical realities but immaterial elements or considerations. As previously discussed here in the study of Christism, the nothing or space must have given off all of its energy or physical force or that something and nothing must have been one if the theory of origin is to be considered in another form or dimension of existence. Regardless that the nothing assumed a position of no energy or force structure, it doesn't mean that it has no force. Its force, although it's greater than the prime mover, is and completely submissive to the force of something; otherwise, if there's no motion that could proceed, all existence is not possible.

Gravitational forces of nature aren't actually fully explainable by science to its very minute details, regardless that its manifestation is obvious to perception. Science is not able to explain its full nature but only calculated and analyzed its mechanics of operations. The effects and source of gravity are apparent, but the actual energy and particle that delivers the force still remains unexplained and undiscovered. Heat and light (electromagnetic radiations) are not the forces responsible for the delivery of gravitational attraction. Science denied the real existence of this force (gravity); although its manifestation is obvious, its physical element couldn't be accounted. A similar situation exists with the attraction and repulsion of like and unlike poles respectively of magnetism, but gravitational force isn't identical with the force of magnetism because magnetism is a force only applicable to polarity of force.

Because the end result of the decomposition of all matter is electromagnetic radiations and energies of sorts, the gravitational and magnetic forces couldn't be attributed to them. In simple analysis the force of gravity should be a force structure that couldn't be subjected to destruction or simplification from its simplest form if it exists as a matter. On this proposition, the law or theory of general relativity is not applicable because the nature of energy constitutes waves and particles, which simply means the accounting of motion—because force is motion—which also means that all matter was created by some form of motion or force. To extend the argument of an indestructible matter or energy structure that supposedly is responsible for is the nemesis of the theory of the black hole.

Even if the black hole event is a concept of elasticity and the reversibility of the theory of general relativity, this episode couldn't happen without the existence of the force of space which is also responsible for the possibility of all motions and creation in the first place. If the prime mover, which is moving itself, is alone, then it must create a space for itself. But the infinity of space couldn't account for how much energy was sacrificed, and it's not even probable to think that energy could have been abolished to eternal nothing to provide the infinite span of nothing. It all seemed that the simplest way to solve the dilemma was to avoid it, because the fact is: there would be no means to explain it by way of materialism.

Even science postulated that the demise of gravitation is a heavy matter that finally discarded itself into nothingness or oblivion. The argument is erroneous because if the nothing or space is made up of heavy matter, then no universal motion could be possible. The argument of a black hole is in itself a concept of materialism which couldn't be rationalized by way of purpose or wisdom because all matter electrons or nuclei are formed by any/some way of energy or force, and all that is formed could be unformed and anything that is unformed could be formed, and it depends on who would do it and under what condition(s). This is supposedly the very thesis of the equation of $E=mc^2$.

If the theological understanding of a prime mover is that moving its creation outside itself will lead into an erroneous speculation, there must be the presence of two distinct material entities involved in the universal phenomena. But on the contrary in the speculation of reality, according to the theory of general relativity, the force/energy equates matter. In other words, there exists a direct bilateral coexistence and reversibility of energy and matter, and they are one force. In fact, science profoundly speculates that the property of light us both a wave and particle, which means that the cause and effect are one inseparable phenomenon. And if there exists a distinct force besides the prime mover, it must be the force of nothing which been introducing its existence with the theory of spiritualism, but the theorist of spiritualism hadn't completely understood its purpose by alienating itself from the concept of materialism.

It must be completely accepted that all matter is only a force structure and has been defined by the theory of general relativity $E=mc^2$. There are two postures of energy: the kinetic and potential. Electromagnetic radiations such as heat and light, etc., are energies in motion, while anything that has mass has a potential energy; however, the relationship of these two energies is reversible. All energy structures are subject to this basic principle at right condition or purpose. Therefore, ***Kinetic energy = Potential energy*** or vice versa, and both must have a degree of one of/or the others at the same time. The theory of general relativity is nothing but a concept of cause and effect. And this concept could be related to Christism's philosophical equation of $r=c/p$. Since matter is only a force/motion/energy structure, all the physical objects of realities we perceive are nothing but the effect of such elements (of cause/force). In the creation of matter, fortunately both the theory of Christism and science believe that the compression or contraction must have been brought about by the mechanielectrochemical process, but the methodology of how the compression or contraction event happened is a diametrical argument between Christism and scientific speculations.

Admitting the theory of general relativity into the theory of Christism would mean that ***reality = Cause and effect/Accounting*** or perception. Based upon this Christism argument, matter is inherently capable of effecting a spirit or perception (thinking). As seen by the theory of the evolution of the species, there are numerous ways upon which perceptions have been produced, notwithstanding that the creator had, by his purpose, structured perceptions evident by the presence of freedom within human beings rather than the evolutionist view that perception is a random act, rather than one that was previously preconceived, of selected or chosen ways and path of lives or events. And if all perceptions have no preconceptions, then God wouldn't have the means of prophecy; also, God could be deceived. The most basic fact to support the notion that all perceptions have been pre-created is that human knowledge will always be limited regardless of its tremendous diversity. The finite human knowledge is relevant to human mortality, which means that God is all-wise. Human thought processes always tend to rationalize (or adhere to coherence), which indicates bounds and parameters between choices so that man always know the difference between evil and good, between selfishness and charity. Man, therefore, didn't invent conscience and morality but lived with/through (chose to obey or deny completely) it (see Structure of Morality for further details) since the beginning of time. Although God knows the beginning and end of everything, he denied such a prerogative or knowledge to humanity because of the purpose of pure exercise of honest faith and freedom.

Matter/creation is nothing but a structure of cause and effect (prime mover/creator), and this fundamental act of creation is evident and manifested equally by the same operational principles from the structure of the atom to the entire universe itself. Even the human being has an excellent understanding of the nature of the atom; man hasn't found the secret of creation even if all acts or the foundation of all creations (even the universe) is in the atomic force structure. The reason of the full understanding of creation isn't available is perhaps due to the fact that the cosmological effect (cause) of creation could only be understood when the whole universal mass is brought under the human microscope/telescope or scrutiny. Not only based upon this assumption but also on the very natures of the most rudimentary energy itself, that the understanding of creation must not be limited or unilaterally accepted by and through the principles of materialism or scientific speculations, especially on the idea that nobody really knows the actual size of the physical universe or universes.

Because the nature of all matter and subatomic or atomic structures are force/energy structure creation, it's therefore evident that the origin of the force must be nonstructured in nature. In the beginning there was no matter. On this basis, the query of which came first (condition) could be answered by the idea that the cause must precede the effect or that an atom couldn't be without electron and proton or the electron and proton of their constituents. Heat and light are two of the most rudimentary forms of energy or force, and their origin is itself a force of motion which could be traced from the question of the origin of the universe itself.

The nature of heat and light is nothing but a force or radiation in wave patterns, which doesn't necessarily constitute a mass but their effect is the most basic need of life. Light, for example, should not necessarily be perceived with a mass; otherwise, it could sustain itself from a source before it is utilized into another form. The effect (chain reaction) of light could be perceived as its mass and conserved or utilized into the metabolism of all living organisms. This process couldn't be stipulated more than the most famous scientific observation of the law of energy conservation (that energy couldn't be created or destroyed). The origin of all things, therefore, is force, and the effect is the structured force as speculated by the theory of general relativity equation as $E=mc^2$, which itself is seemingly just another look at the law of conservation of energy but states its reversibility.

Because truth could only commence from a valid foundation or from the nearest assumption, hence, philosophy as well as science has a very basic foundation for the basis of initiation for the quest of the final truth. Therefore, in Christism (as a foundation of truth) a unified concept of the nature of the universe must be seen with a trinitarian identity or existence: 1) God the Father, the nothing or the immaterial creator; 2) God the son, the matter or the semi and full-structured force; 3) The Holy Spirit, the knowledge or purpose. To fully understand the future evens such as human salvation for immortality, it must begin with a concept that space, time, and motion/force are inseparable immortal universal realities so that one couldn't exist without the other with a homogenous spirit with each other. In other words, the nothing, force, and spirit are one and a unified reality, and we call this universal phenomena or creation.

One universal phenomenon is the existence of human beings with two major present realities: life and death. These human enigmas are a perception of the gods themselves. All perceptions and behaviors of human beings revolve within these two realities. Immortality, a reality which presently only belongs to the gods, became a pursuit of human perception. Because all perceptions were preconceived by God, immortality therefore

71

is a path or future event to be chosen, not mandated or coerced, because perception is always a choice or liberty; otherwise, its purpose will cease. Therefore, only those who choose immortality will have immortality. But that choice must always be a way that remains conditional through the structure of morality. Because all life activities do all possess force/energy process expenditure as speculated by the concept of materialism, hence, every act of humanity is recorded by God, who himself is The Force. Therefore, there's no human action or behavior that could possibly escape from the spirit or knowledge of God.

To completely understand universal phenomena, the enigma or gravitational force must be construed by the notion that the nothing is queued to all creation; otherwise, no life and existence is possible. The consideration of immortality couldn't only be a decision based upon the action of energy/force or matter alone because perception is not possible without life, and without the nothing there's no life. In other words, even the gravitational force is perceived as an action of matter, regardless that there is no material explanation of it (gravity). Gravitation, therefore, is a bilateral (mutual) interaction of the nothing and something for the purpose of physical existence, because universal existence depends completely on this force—i.e., the light from the sun. Even the Big Bang theorist postulated that gravitational force (causing explosion and/or implosion of sorts) was responsible for the universal phenomena.

Every concept of immortality must be a unified action of all the three forces of existence because all perception is a unified front of these three realities based upon the concept that thinking or spirit is an energy process, and all energy processes have their origins from the creator (nothing) and are continuously perpetuated by the something (the law of conservation of energy) as perceived—by humans—as the cause and effect or matter. It's not possible to assume that the totality of universal mass could be derived by the mere calculation of gravitational force or motion applied or exerted upon the solar system. In other words, universal phenomena couldn't be fully construed by human accounting or truth alone by way of material calculation. Therefore, it's not possible to completely know how God thinks or processes his knowledge except that the force is in all living organisms and is the cause of all human thinking possible because energy is a chain reaction process or a domino effect.

The knowledge of immortality, therefore, is relevant to perception. Because life is a perception of God, mortality is also, and without death immortality has no meaning nor is there a human perception about God or the creator. And through the structure of morality, the perception of the existence of evil is a direct result as an anomaly in the struggle of life preservation (see Structure of Morality).

The Judeo-Christian Scripture itself admitted the fact that selfishness was the root of all evil. Human existence is based on perception by both the creator and humanity, and every individual is given the privilege or liberty of individual freedom of such to determine his/her own faith and fate or destiny. As has been promulgated in Christism, *reality = creation /perception*. This philosophical equation is what the determinant of present reality as well as the future events of immortality because all events are perceptions of the Creator.

Did God create evil then? Indeed, the paths and ways of evil are there, but the choice to enter such commission of evil acts is completely dependent on every' individual for there's no coercion on the part of God. Regardless that human social behavior managers are trying hard to restrict individual freedom and liberty, it would never be possible, for death is the only viable solution that could completely imprison the will of the human mind. The notion that freedom/liberty is perception, and by the same token perception is not possible without freedom, likewise no freedom no life, because freedom is life, so motion is life. and without the nothing or void there's no motion; therefore, without nothing there's no life. If immortality is the ultimate preservation of life, then the nothing (creator) must remain to have a great contribution.

In the present human reality, the most dominant perception of every individual is self-preservation. Self-preservation is never evil;

in fact, it's the motivation a precursor of immortality. Unfortunately, it also became the weakness of every individual is very much evident with biblical expressions such as "everyone has sinned and come short of the glory of God" and "we are all sinners before the sight of God." The perception of self-preservation will be completely eliminated because it would be homogenized to the perception of immortality; hence, sin would be completely eliminated. Because sin and mortality are a perception, immortality is also a perception. Therefore, when God changes his perception for his creation from mortality' to immortality, then the knowledge and reality of human dimension will respond to the purpose of immortality. In the best analysis, when the perception of God will change. creation and reality will be changed, and any philosophical or scientific notions will be completely invalidated. The perception of mortality and immortality couldn't come at the same dispensation of a dimension of reality because, as has been explored in this study about the purpose of mortality, immortality should be preceded by mortality. So, due to the present dispensation of the perception (human mortality) of God, humanity doesn't have a real clue (technical knowledge) of anything about immortality or how it could be done because all human wisdom on the present dispensation is practically limited to a mortality dimension. Therefore, any real philosophical and material understanding of immortality will elude all human endeavors and undertakings except pure philosophical speculations; however, any speculation's relationship to probability is only relevant upon its arguments, and the reception and admission to one's perception of truth must be upon every individual choice alone. However, (philosophically) it's imperative to stipulate that regardless of the sequential relationship of mortality and immortality events that should take place, all life experiences during the tenure of the mortality state must be retained (as read-only memory) in the immortality reality. In other words, as the dimension of immortality take place, the benefit must be retroactive to all living beings since the foundation of creation as it has been stipulated as the resurrection of the righteous dead by the theology of the Judeo-Christian Scriptures.

As previously mentioned, the practical purpose of why mortal beings does not have the knowledge of the technical (material) aspect of immortality is based on the ramification on the issue of freedom itself and secondarily on the basis of learning and acknowledging the nature and purposes of the creator. To post a real heavy philosophical or scientific scrutiny about whether immortality is possible is not only to study the nature but also on the argument that human knowledge about the real origin of energy or force itself, by which such notion has been presented in this study. The real issue, therefore, is not whether immortality is possible but whether there's a possibility of the existence of God or a creator, which is an issue of cause and effect, which means that God is the cause and immortality is the effect because, on the ultimate analysis, if there's God, there would be immortality.

Regardless that a lot of propositions, speculations, and even physical evidence have been presented in this study of Christism about the possibility of the existence of a creator or God, it's imperative to answer why science or the philosophical concept of materialism rejects the idea or notion of the very existence of a creator and also why a lot of religious beliefs and faiths attribute immortality or God only on the realm of spiritual existence. If a valid argument could be provided to answer these questions, then the probability of the existence of God could be beyond dispute.

Since the foundation of human history and thereafter the two greatest philosophical arguments that surfaced about the nature of existence are science and religion or materialism and spiritualism. Both of these schools of thought basically possess truth in their respective arguments. Unfortunately, both philosophies inherently deny the other's thesis, which brought about their weakness, calamity, and corruption. The influences of these two great pillars of thought or thesis are what made up the consciousness of the present general society in a worldwide proportion. As these two forces collide in every aspect of human life, their effects are obviously multifaceted from the making of robotic moralism to unimaginable possessions of material selfishness. Because as long as we teach ourselves with false doctrines, the perception of human beings will always have the tendency of the immediate requirement of physical survival Why? Because it's the primary requirement of God as stipulated in the study of the structure of morality. On the contrary, religion has been in denial of this fact by teaching immortality of the soul, self-sacrifice, self-denial, condemnation of worldliness, pilgrimage, fastings, celibacy, etc.

The contrast between materialism and spiritualism sharpens, as the materialist aggrandizes himself with great power and glorious material possession and as the spiritualist relegates blame and all sins and transgressions as desires of the flesh. Even the robotic moralist will win of the battle for the complete destruction of the free will of humanity through and by the use of the mechanics of fulfilling the material cravings of individuals or their subjects. At some point there will be a revival of freedom before salvation will come; salvation must be only for those who have chosen and the exceptions of God. But if materialism will win in the next century, the mortality might increase because materialism admits no salvation from his mortality. But both philosophies appeal to emotion. For spiritualism, the immortality of the soul, and for the materialist, complete the denial of a creator, are a mechanism of escapism.

Materialism as well as spiritualism both possess some degree of truth in and of themselves, except that they lack the insight of the whole truth. Obviously, materialism is a concept that doesn't embrace any relevance of the immaterial part of existence or universal reality, thereby accepting the notion that there's no creator or God and that all existence has no purpose. The materialist has no clear understanding of matter and thereby assigns for the sake of philosophical expediency that space also constitutes matter that it couldn't be accounted for by any sense or perception. Materialists, therefore. partly deceive themselves by attributing physical mass property of the void/nothing or space just for the of expediency in filling a philosophical inadequacy. Materialists failed to have recognized the true implication of the two natures of universal force: non-structured (nothing/space); semi-structured (emf radiation [light]) and structured (mass).

The philosophy of materialism has much relevance and significance. One is that it provides a check to restrict religious/spiritual the extremism-like denial of the desires of the flesh. especially sexual, which is essential for a species preservation discussed in the structure of morality. Second the concept that matter has no value and purpose by itself because of the idea that matter created itself alone; also, it needed immortality dependent upon another.

The overall spirit of matter (son of God) of its desperation of immortality is self-evident with the concept of materialism. The fiasco of the materialist is that instead of seeking or understanding that the salvation of matter relies on something immaterial, it has attributed all existence to matters, thereby it became completely selfish. This explains the phenomenon of human selfishness as the root of all evil. Because the philosophy of materialism became not only confined to logic and physical sciences but adapted into human lifestyles, it all seemed that the attributes and origin of sin are spiritual in the human dimension (because of philosophy), but its other origin is the matter (universal physical existence) itself which is trying to communicate its real nature that matter has been created by God the father (the nothing) and its life and immortality is of God the father—the nothing or space. Unfortunately, the message or spirit of matter has been misunderstood.

Utilizing the Christism philosophical equation of $r=c/p$ it's easy to recognize that the origin of evil reality in human beings is its perception of the nature of matter. The concept of materialism (not in a form of written or expressed philosophy) had existed (pre-medieval or medieval form) in the mind of the first sinner when the first act of sin took place. Because nobody really could document when the first act of sin was committed, the Judeo-Christian stipulation about the origin of evil is itself attributed to the act of selfishness. Materialism's philosophical debacle probably ushered in the modern concept of selfishness even to the present human era because of the tremendous advances of technology propagated by physical sciences. In fact, modem physics still clings to the practice of attributing physical properties to the nature of space. The full understanding of the nature of space, therefore, is the only way which determines whether God or a creator exists because it's impossible that matter might have created itself by itself and could exist by itself alone. Materialism perceived creation unilaterally to constitute all matter and therefore arrived with the concept or reality that there's no God or creator. The spirit of materialism as well as spiritualism preexisted with the creation of human beings, but it has various degrees of manifestations ((ancient) because all transgressions (misuse of selfishness) couldn't possibly occur without cause and effect as expressed by the equation $r=c/p$.

But whether the sin of the misuse of selfishness occurred, humanity still will continue to experience mortality because, as it has been stipulated here in this study, immortality couldn't be appreciated without the experience of mortality or just the knowledge of it. Sin occurred as evidence of the preexistence of the free will of man; however, sin is not a mechanism for the causation of the consciousness of the free will of man because it's only the misuses or restrictions of freedom that result in transgressions.

It's now become self-evident that materialists couldn't prove the existence of God through the existence of matter alone, because it's not possible by any ultimate stretch of logical reasoning. The final downfall and destruction of materialism is its profound sense of selfishness on the basis or on the fact that it's so self-evident that the nature of space/nothing could never be explained it concluded that the mystery couldn't be the possibility of the existence of a creator. In other words, materialists completely misunderstood the spirit and message of matter or the son of God. But nobody should condemn materialists of final judgment, for the act of salvation is the sole prerogative of God.

The failure, and what could have been the salvation of materialists, lies in a very thin line of argument. A materialist could be analyzed as one who took his own victory or defeat for the sake of not living under any cloak of guilt. The materialist, therefore, understood the absolute glory of the denial of any possibility of the existence of a creator or God; thereby he thought he created himself and he is the God or creator–the theory of the Big Bang–and the Judeo-Christian Bible understood the argument posted that Lucifer is the most magnificent archangel of God in heaven who was cast out because of his selfishness and pride in wanting to be God.

The origin of the concept of spirit (good) of materialism existed during the creation, but humanity exhibited bad responses with the message. Because materialism, like spiritualism, must be inherent in all human motivation with the structure of morality, it's not unusual to believe that the misuse of selfishness is as old as human civilization itself. As the whole universal physical reality (matter) itself manifests its own self-preservation mechanism, likewise every human inherently possesses the same responsibility. Astrology is a temptation to bridge the connection between human behavior with universal phenomena, but this concept is also limited and is not credible enough for the reason that the spirit of the gods must be in all creation so that life or existence is possible. It must be stipulated that astrology itself must be just another variation of materialism. The spirit and wisdom of the gods must be agreeable to DNA modalities to following the freedom and decision of every human's individual righteous and evil act. The gods respect absolute free will but not that the consequences (good or bad) aren't known. This is absolute justice of God.

Spiritualism is a concept that has an origin from God the father himself: the nothing or space. His message or spirit is his absolute immortality and immaterial physical reality. Not that some human didn't recognize the phenomenon, but it's the misuse and misunderstanding that proliferated: for example, some spiritualists actually believe that the human soul is immortal, and the spirit of the deceased is in the other dimension of immortal reality. Others perform self-homicide to transfer their physical reality to the other dimension. Spiritualism (good or bad) itself is as old as human civilization, as evident in the practice of religious ceremonies of ancient tribes. In fact, the Christian Scripture preaching of the human creation at the Garden of Eden is a concept or a direct affair of God and man.

But interestingly enough, the debacle or downfall of spiritualism is inherent in its own message and directly analogous with the failure of materialism. The failure of spiritualism lies in its misuse of the real implication of the message from God the father (the nothing). Immortality of the soul became a message for the human spirit after death, thereby furnishing himself with an exclusive attribute of nature of God the father. In fact, the Judeo-Christian Scripture in the book of Genesis provided the origin of spiritualism on the scene of the temptation of Eve by the serpent in the Garden of Eden: "ye shall not surely die." It's obvious that both the debacle of materialism and spiritualism lies in humanity's robbing the gods of their intended message about their nature. In the most fundamental argument, spiritualism (misused) failed to have recognized the purpose of creation. As it has been stipulated here in this study of Christism, the ultimate purpose of the deity is the creation of the physical universe, including all life in it. Any proposition or belief of immortality for humanity must therefore allow physical reality to submit reason to the purpose of the creator; otherwise, the commission of self-deception of the real truth is afforded.

The question of why truth is not readily fed into every human consciousness is an aspect of disregarding the profound sense of the purpose of freedom and responsibility; otherwise, in the fullest extent of the argument, humans should have been just a robot of God. Actually, human mortality as a present, temporary reality must be looked at with the issues and ramifications of the purpose so that immortality could find rationality. And as a case in point, the coming (time appointed) immortality shouldn't be a proposition of humanity. Even the Judeo-Christian biblical logic didn't actually set an absolute time capsule of the second coming of Jesus Christ. In fact, it offered a more likely stipulation that it (he) will come like a thief in the night.

Human individual salvation must therefore follow the protocol of responsibility with respect to the structure of morality, and every individual must have the full freedom to choose or select what is the absolute truth and not with any insinuation of coercion. In fact, the Christian Scripture itself stipulated that the path to salvation is a very narrow road, which should mean that God would take into consideration major human perceptions about creation.

With the discussion for the consideration about responsibility for individual salvation for immortality, the misuse of both the concept of spiritualism and materialism is the major determinant. The structure of morality presented with this study is comprehensive enough for the balanced exercise where both materialism and spiritualism blend together. Materialism is actually a very broad conceptual spirit with its origin and source from the Son of God or the matter itself, but its end result must be the preservation of life or physical existence (including universal physical reality). On the other hand, the real concept of spiritualism is the manifestation of the presence of immaterial force or reality which is responsible for all physical existence, and its message is also a preservation of what he had created. Such a preservation will extend to be provided with immortality in an appointed time schedule. The structure of morality presented in this study is a guide to this phenomenon for the reason that God would act on purpose and not by mere chance, although reason dictates that there will always be exceptions.

Materialism and spiritualism shouldn't be separated from and hostile to one of the other. The combination of the two is the result of the universal existence. Just like an atom of sodium combined with an atom of chlorine to produce a molecule of salt, in such a combination the salt has a distinct property from that of sodium and chlorine alone.

81

This illustrates the trinitarian nature of universal reality as exemplified in the trinitarian nature of human being. In the universal reality, the origin of the force was God he father or the space or nothing before it became a complete nothing. And such a force or cause produced all the matter of effects as the universal physical reality. As long as the nothing (God the father) will not retrieve back the force, the universe will remain in constant motion. This perpetual motion is primarily due to what became immaterial in nature (zero energy/zero mass) of space, thereby its interaction with the matter doesn't utilize energy consumption. The materialist had seen the effect of such interactions and therefore attributed everything to matter for the reason that the force (cause) behind the effect has no material manifestation whatsoever. All matter, atomic and subatomic particles, motions and thoughts have material manifestations seen as effects or actions, push or pull. EMF radiations are all effects, as are gravitational forces, but in the origin of the initial force, since it delivered its effect, became a chain of reversible reactions seen even by the most famous scientific equation $E=mc^2$ and it became a perpetual force. God the father, the nothing (pre-absolute space or nothing state) who delivered the original initial force constantly maintains its creation by holding the whole, huge, universal physical phenomena in its place within the infinite span of space.

Absolute truth, therefore, must be a true derivative a perception of the whole cosmic creation of phenomena, including the phenomenon of absolute infinite span of nothing or immaterial space. This deduction of truth is comprehensively expressed by the Christism philosophical equation $r=c/p$. wherein creation could be perceived on an individual basis, regardless that it might produce similar results or reality with other preceptors. Likewise, the deity might have used this same principle in a rudimentary form, which resulted with humanity's transient mortality reality state. And with the same token, the salvation of individual should be based upon this principle $(r=c/p)$, which is a dynamic force in constant play with human motivation and response mechanisms as seen in human behavior, lifestyle, or personal philosophy of life.

Since all human behavior has partial or full material (effects) manifestations or components. it's therefore ignorant or antagonistic to offer opposition to the notion that God is capable of recording the major human actions necessary for the issuance of immortality. Perhaps the greatest enigma is the notion of whether immortality of the flesh and procreation (love and sex) could coexist at the same time. This concept is actually expressed by the reversibility of the equation $E=mc^2$, but as for immortality of the soul (pure spiritualism) such a theory is disproven by materialism that the attribute of the physical genetic component is the modulation upon which the unique identity of the individual has been issued. Regardless that the scientific notation $E=mc^2$ might be true, the concept of immortality of the soul (spirit alone without material component) are far from being verifiable as reality. The only viable way upon which reincarnation is possible is with the notion that the human spirit is encoded with the atom or even subatomic particles postmortem.

Even when taking everything into consideration, one solid fact of human reality is mortality. The Judeo-Christian Scripture stipulated a concept of immortality which by itself also denied the technical aspect of consideration. Because human life couldn't possibly exist without the appetite for the truth, because every human reality or activity is itself a result of perception (internal or external), the proposition of philosophical or otherwise is a necessary component of existence. One of the greatest scientific theories that had stood throughout the ages is the principle of the conservation of energy. If immortality is of the flesh, then the enigma with its coexistence of procreation (love and sex) must revolve with the principle of energy conservation. And for the sake of theoretical and not of detailed technical propriety, a certain cutoff is necessary within each genealogy as the cycle of procreation ends and restarts so that each generation will actually exactly repeat itself, meaning that every individual has its own precise rebirth at an appointed time. However, this phenomenon could only happen when God changes his perception of creation to immortality. This is the theory of homogenous perception. Absolute freedom, therefore, would be no longer available in the new immortal dimension because reality becomes permanent and perception becomes homogenous, preventing the possibility of evil. Therefore, the individual who would be blessed to be selected in the new immortal dimension of permanent reality and had chosen righteousness from the previous mortal dimension of temporary reality would be considered as a seed of a new immortal generation. The theory of energy conservation would be reconciled by the modality of the cutoff of every cycle of every genealogy. The modality of marriage in the immortal dimension of reality would be completely predestined to protect exact rebirth of every individual; thereby, each generation would be a precise restatement from a previous event effecting the recycling of the same consciousness.

The philosophical equation $r=c/p$ in the immortal dimension of permanent reality would be revised and converted into a non-variable equation which translates that creation and recreation would be completely a product of homogenous perception of the trinitarian deity with all creatures. In the immortal state of permanent reality, mortality would be limited only to natural death to be dictated by the course of the application of the principle of energy conservation: that procreation is limited to the amount of allowable energy available, so that a cutoff is required to end and begin the cycle of each genealogy.

Perhaps the greatest inquiry is whether the immortal permanent reality is a state of robotic perception or morality. Because God will always be a Creator of reason, any memory of good or evil during the previous mortality dimension is only retrievable as "read-only memory," which means that it couldn't be used or activated because all active perceptions in the immortal permanent dimension are according to righteousness of submission to God's will, which means that all perception is homogenous to God's perception or perception is completely an integral part of creation. In a simple deduction of reason, in the immortal permanent reality, humans would start a new lesson of life, regardless that all past life experiences in the mortal temporary reality is available as read-only memory; in simple reasoning, the past (read-only memory) and the would-be present immortal dimensions of reality merge together to issue relevance to the perfect character of God, which means that living in the immortal dimension would be completely cherished and acclaimed from or with the point of view of the past experiences in the previous mortal dimension of reality.

The dilemma of the retention of the anatomy and physiology of a human in the mortal dimension into the immortal dimension must be adjudged with the initial intent and purpose of the Creator, as has been discussed according to the structure of morality. Human perception and metabolism, therefore, must be carried as two entities with indispensable collaboration into the immortal dimension regardless that mortality would be limited or confined (to natural mortality) by the dictates and functions of the principle of energy conservation, which means that the amount of available energy for recycling would be relative to how much genealogy would be processed at one time and at what life span an individual would survive during his own genealogical period.

The mortality period or event in the immortal dimension shouldn't be confused with our present reality. If a simple comparative analysis with the aforementioned proposition in the immortal dimension against our present mortal reality, it would be very conspicuous that we aren't at any degree at immortal dimension or reality. One good explanation is that the present dimension, our mortality is not limited to natural death; second, a complete mortal dimension (as a learning process of faith and election–which would benefit immortality–by the creator) must precede the immortal dimension reality. It must be fully understood that regardless of a certain time span mortality must be necessary in the immortal dimension. The mortal period is not a mortal dimension. The word *dimension* must be understood as a complete and whole reality and is not just a part of a reality, which means that mortality is only a transitional part of reality in the immortal dimension of reality; therefore it's just a component of the whole predominant process.

If one is to deny the absolute material relationship of the collaboration of the coexistence of immortality and metabolism as the only method by which a perception could possibly take place is to surrender one's faith and beliefs to the concept of full immortality of the soul, which has no prerequisite or need of the flesh or matter for its existence. With this assumption, then reality would be completely restricted to the nature of God the Father (the immaterial or nothing). But one could only fool oneself without presenting an answer to the question: why did God in the first place create a physical universe with a physical human existence?

The materialism concept that thoughts and perceptions have material components must purposely be not only the valid but also the only possible way of physical existence and also the only method by which God could communicate and record all human activity for the purpose of awarding immortality. Although this process of God's communication and connection couldn't be recognized by human perception and senses, it's the only mechanism by which human salvation for immortality and physical existence is viable; this process is easily reconciled to the notion that the nature of God the son which ranges from semi-structured (light) subatomic to the most gigantic cosmic energy force structure (universal mass [matter]).

The concept in Christism that the sin of the misuse of the truth or real message behind materialism and spiritualism must be fully understood for the complete and absolute comprehension of how and what is the nature of existence in the coming immortal dimension of reality. And to effectuate such physical immortal reality must be the work of the Son of God. As the Judeo-Christian Scripture stipulated that the salvation/redemption of man was and would be the work of Jesus Christ who was willing to have sacrificed (died) himself for humanity. This message is relevant in the immortal dimension of reality by which God the son (cosmic Christ/matter) will have full control of the management of the exact and precise recycling of every genealogy so that every action of birth and rebirth of each generation will not allow a degree of the misapplication or corruption of energy. Therefore, perfection is a must in the immortal dimension of reality in order to effectuate a precise rebirth of every individual which means that every individual must be marrying the same individual to give birth to the same offspring at each cycle or event of the eternal recycling of each genealogy. This event is possible because God's and humanity's perceptions would be homogenous. In other words, the philosophical equation $r=c/p$ would become $r=(c+p)$, which means that human perception (also freedom) has a limited set of parameters or boundaries which are controlled by the will of God. In a simple declaration, perception would be confined to only one direction of action or motive, which is righteousness, which is the very will of God. Learning itself becomes just an acceptance and execution of the perfect will of God.

Regardless that the complete detail of the technical aspect of immortality is not available, it's only because we are living in the mortal dimension of reality, and so mortality is at the very immediate explanation of human knowledge in a sense that even the very destruction of the atom has become possible. However, in this mortal dimension we have a prediction of immortality, such as the notion that our spirit is immortal; such a case is correct for the reason that every individual action is being recorded by the son of God (the matter) for the purpose of who will receive the blessing of immortality and who will be allocated the eternal destruction we call hell. But even if humans have perception of an immortal spirit, it shouldn't be confused with the sin of spiritualism, which believe that the spirit of man could actually exist by itself and as immortal somewhere after death. This notion will destroy the eternal purpose of God for the coming immortality of physical existence. It is only God the father (space/nothing) who has the possibility of full eternal spiritual or immaterial existence. This dilemma has been argued by the Judeo-Christian Scripture in the book of Genesis during the temptation of Eve: "ye shall not surely die" and "ye shall be as gods" (Genesis 3:4, Genesis 3:5).

What Is Truth?

The theory of Christism doesn't attempt to impose itself an absolute prediction of the future for the ultimate that it's only an act of arrogance or self-deception to make believe that we could actually know the will of God while we are at the dispensation or living in a mortal dimension. But any attempt to forbid the liberty for the understanding and the dissemination of such understanding of one's personal (inspired or what have you) perception and concept of the nature of creation and believe that it wouldn't be condemned (by reason or God) is an absolute act or manifestation of arrogance and tyranny.

The absolute fact that we are living in the mortal dimension is of the notion that a unified or homogenous perception of the truth is not possible. but this impossibility is itself a part of the truth for the understanding that a truth is forthcoming, such as whether there will be immortality or that creation is just a complete act of an accidental episode as seen by the theorist of unilateral materialism—that there's no God. Faith, therefore, is the jurisdiction of truth, and as has been stipulated in this study of Christism, faith is a perception of an unseen creator such as God the father, the nothing or space. The strength of faith must be relevant upon the general implication of what is perceived whether it be material or immaterial. And if everything is material (as the materialist believes) then there's no need for faith and truth because truth is a component of what is and is not; e.g., color is only relevant according to the different bands or wavelengths or spectrums of light so that green is distinguishable from yellow and not just by nomenclature or etymology but by the actual deferential of physical property, but the coded nomenclature is purely spiritual regardless that it's completely necessary and effective.

Man's inherent desire for truth is as ancient as the first instinct to study—with the materialistic aspect—the matter or the nature of human environment and/or his own nature. Therefore, the fact that man possesses perception itself and/or his own leads man to the confirmation of truth. Hence the dilemma turns upside down: how could there be no God or purpose? Knowledge, therefore, has no option of advancement if there's no purpose, and any quest of purpose is the seeking of/for reality or truth. Even unilateral materialism couldn't possibly attribute any truth to himself if the whole universal existence does all consist of matter because the natural impulse of truth that drives perception couldn't proceed in such a condition. In a simple deduction, the materialist does believe in an accidental episode of creation by the matter itself had happened or could actually happen so that it attributed a physical property of space as an immaterial matter, that all space within or outside the universal mass does consist of immaterial matter or untouchable matter. But such a notion or opinion is an escapism of reality and couldn't possibly discard the dilemma of proving the question of the infinity of space. It's obvious if seen from a purely philosophical point of view; it's outright selfishness and self-deception because it's a complete denial of the absolute clarity of definition which is a demand of truth itself. Even the act of denial of truth is itself a part of the truth to imply that truth does really exist, because how does one know which side he advocates? For an extension even for advocacy must be a matter of choice, and choice itself could only be conceived from two sides. Even in the final outstretch of reason, even if the materialist's concept is a truth solely to himself, the fact that he derived a truth for himself is direct evidence that truth exists; therefore, purpose or truth couldn't possibly be a pure derivative of a chance. Evil, therefore, is just an argument of misconception (or a misguided perception of creation) of the absolute truth that is the primary causation of inappropriate and complete selfish behavior and actions.

Truth also stands on the basis of pure choice of which is the right and wrong perception. Truth must come with the origin of perception is itself unknown with the fact that even a single-celled organism does possess a certain sense of purpose or perception—because matter itself is a purpose. Even choice in and of itself is a purpose. It's therefore a deducible verity to say that origin is a purpose. An extension of this concept, such as the singularity theory of the Big Bang, must have occupied a space outside itself, and such a space must be an immaterial force which has a direct effect on how the whole universal mass could stay afloat and be created and have a definite mass and definite location amidst an infinite span of immaterial space. All concepts of origin, therefore, must accommodate the consideration of a space both within and outside itself. It's only upon such a concept that the presence or existence of an immaterial force and material reality that perception, knowledge, purpose, choice, philosophy, accounting, etc., is made possible. Outside of this argument, even any argument couldn't possibly exist. Therefore, God is origin because we know the truth by way of philosophy as well as the understanding of physical nature of the universe by way of the study of Christism or any similar venture: because there's no concrete justification that matter could exist by itself and everything is matter, and the human is able to understand that matter is matter. The sin of spiritualism and unilateral must always be seen as a self-deception of the truth. Is it coincidental that the opposite of truth is deception? Or is it self-evident that an immaterial force is alive and in existence and holds the whole universe it created in space? The choice is ours whether to believe matter didn't create itself alone. This is faith: that God the father, before he became completely nothing or an immaterial space, created (with and by a purpose) the universal physical existence and all that is in it, as has been stipulated in this study of Christism to understand the possibility of the existence of absolute truth.

The Judeo-Christian Scripture itself presented one of the most brilliant assertions about the effect of having the truth "Ye shall know the truth and the truth shall make you free." In simple analysis, an individual argument could only have a choice of several things under consideration in order for one concept to be free to his own opinion from another's. So, all consideration and relevance for the existence of truth is the existence of knowledge of whatever form which is the issue of choice which itself forms the truth. Truth, therefore, is physical existence in itself. the nature of God and their purposes.

The study and pursuit of Christism does not by any means have any intention to engage any form of contention with any form of religious or cultural beliefs. but serves to present an alternative or enhancement to existing ideologies or tenets for the sole purpose of the furtherance of faith for the truth of the probability of the existence of divine creator and to provide humanity more of a chance for preservation on the idea that there is a God who does exist and who's choosing righteous individual (according to the Structure of morality and God's aspect of forgiveness) to whom will be imparted the blessing of salvation and who shall be the seeds in the coming new dimension of immortal reality. In the commencement of the immortal dimension everyone would become a virgin (to enter the immortal dimension one must be undefile-this would be the work of God the son [matter]) to be married and to start a new immortal genealogy.

The philosophy of Christism doesn't claim a special divine inspiration but rather believes that whosoever seeketh the truth seeketh God, for truth is God and God is the truth. "I am the way, the truth, and the life" states a profound text from the Christian Bible. But what's the truth that is God's? Any form of revelation with the concept that guides one toward the ultimate or immortal preservation of universal physical creation of reality is considered the absolute truth that is of God. And whosoever holds the truth and exercises the structure of morality would be included in such a final fate of the ultimate purpose of God. Truth, therefore, bears faith and responsibility in the present tenure of the present mortal temporary reality, and all honest seekers of philosophical or scientific knowledge will culminate in the ultimate purpose of immortality in some form.

The sin of materialism and spiritualism is the most fundamental evidence that truth leadeth one to his own choice of deception from or conversion to the truth. The magnificent nature of the justice of God is for the permission of the truth to be manipulated to all possible modalities as the very means of God's capability for precise election for the blessing of immortality. Therefore, there is no possibility of the concept of innocent indulgences of transgressions because the misuse of selfishness (materialism) leads to the denial of charity and compassion. Extreme selfishness couldn't possibly be committed without a degree of self-deception of the innate impulse of acquiescence and conscience. The sin of the misuse of selfishness couldn't even be justified by the theory of evolution that all human instincts are with animal origin because the motive of extreme selfishness itself is glorification of the self. If evidence is to be presented, then when did we ever see a rich man cohabitating with the hogs or living with all sorts of animals in the barn? After all, how much more animalistic could a human become if not for extreme selfishness? Is it more logical to believe that Adolf Hitler was trying to be an animal or god in his own rationale? In fact, the parable of the prodigal son in the Christian Scripture is quite interesting for highlighting the dilemma of the situation.

The truth is very much self-evident, even with the sin of materialism itself, because the rich man didn't revert to the barn but rather, with all desires, built palaces for himself which is an indication of a desire for the best of everything. The very nature of the necessity of selfishness is actually the impulse for the spirit of immortality (given by God at creation); it's only the misuse that could cause a backlash that could drive an individual or the whole society to be deceived and doubtful of the immortal truth. The truth of God already provided in our human nature and with the whole physical phenomena itself (that every creature and creation have a preset perception of parameters as that a species begat its own). The truth is a driver impulse for perception and investigation (philosophical or scientific) of creation, and during the process one would either deny or reach a conclusion or confirmation of the truth and make a declaration then abide in it through faith. This natural phenomenon is expressed in Christism as the philosophical equation $r=c/p$. It is analogous to the concept that no one could tell a lie without first committing a self-deception. In a very simple derivative, it's impossible to tell a lie without knowing it, or a simpler extension of the idea is that all lies couldn't be performed without premeditation; otherwise. the human brain (and God the son universal physical matter) would have no record of the event. Otherwise, it wasn't a lie at all but a random inadvertent error. In like manner with the truth that if it doesn't have a very conclusive foundation or confirmation within an individual's perception, it wouldn't result in the obedience of the structure of morality; therefore, the misuse of selfishness is allowed to be exercise and the act of faith is without real piety, but all subordinated to the misuse of self-preservation.

Because there's only one creator, there's only one truth. The driver impulse of truth is identically provided to all human beings, but it's the element of choice (freedom) and perception (ability) that are the variables. However, the end or ultimate result remains identical as either an act of righteousness or deception, either the confirmation of the belief in the existence of God or the contrary. But it's not the fact that other individuals could arrive at the conclusion that there's no God that determines whether there's God or not, it's rather the process of determination and confirmation or investigation (denial or acceptance) that must confirm whether there's a truth or God.

The theory of Christism's declaration of truth centered on the enigma of reality: the consideration of the interrelationships of mortality, metabolism, perception, nature of deity (gods), and immortality. It's evident that study and quests of physics and related sciences, metaphysical sciences, and philosophy or reason are only relevant with value in the prospect of the existence or non-existence of God. A case in point in science is an attempt to produce immortality from the laboratory, but even such a laboratory venture for immortality couldn't possibly avoid dealing with the dilemma of metabolism which includes the issues but is not limited to procreation, energy conservation–the limit of energy available, and, of course, the immortal preservation of every individual unique spirit or consciousness of knowing himself as himself forever. On the other hand, spiritualism will always be busy deceiving itself that the spirits of their dead do exist and has yet to make an exposition of the existence of such spirits. Even the faith of Judeo-Christians must answer with the degree of some responsibility of the complete diametrical nature of the season (miracles) of events of the believed biblical historical reality with the present human era. In simple analysis, therefore, the imposition of any faith and belief system must never be conducted with any form of coercion, regardless of moral or economic objectives, even in such a case that such a faith claims divine inspiration.

In Christism divine (general) inspiration is the driver impulse that is present in all human beings that leads to the perception of creation for the confirmation or denial of the truth, and such perception is awarded with absolute freedom that may witness the justice of a creator. Truth, therefore, with all its ramification has preexistence in all creation and through human perception of creation itself determines an individual reality and behavior that leads to one's own salvation through the election of God. The theory of Christism established the human connection and consciousness with his creator, as the very nature of all creation itself, as the union of both matter (the son of God) and immaterial force (God the father) according to their purpose as having created the physical universal reality and all the creatures in it.

Perhaps one of the most basic and fundamental elements of evidence that could also support the argument of inherent general revelation of truth in all human beings is the fact of the order or ascension of knowledge itself such that worship to God took precedence just prior to the advancement of astronomy and then physics and biological sciences.

This series of episodes of human enlightenment are also an assertion of the coherence which is the very nature of divine truth.

Many forms of religion and worship had existed as the direct evidence of the freedom of choice imparted to every human perception, but not only on the nature of the perception (response) of the truth but also of the element of its honesty and intent that will have a significant impact upon the salvation of the individual. Of course, God could always exercise the prerogative of the issuance of exemptions.

There are only two possible concepts about the nature of God. One is the separatist concept, as has been stipulated earlier in this study, which is the most prevalent form of perception as manifested in the numerous religious sects and organizations. Many, if not all, religions have a declaration of faith based upon the concept that God is a spirit that has a capability toward physical transformation from one form to any other form of existence (such as in the form of a human being, etc.) in no time, but such a claim couldn't possibly be documented or have a viability to be documented or confirmed in any form in the present era. Such a mystical assertion of the nature of God has a tremendous contribution and merit in the upbringing of morality in human consciousness and behavior to a lot of segments of society, regardless of the issue of its highly doubtful absolute truthfulness. And if God will promulgate exception for salvation on the believers–honesty and intent–of spiritualism, then so, at the sole of discretion of the creator, the truth must be at the full understanding of human beings and not in any way be influenced by God himself; otherwise, it would defy the justice of his own character and intent of election for immortality in philosophical justice, as stipulated by the Judeo-Christian Scripture on the issue of the "priesthood of all believers."

The only other major concept of the nature of God is the idea that God's nature and existence is the whole universal physical reality (Cosmic Christ) as the union (interaction) of matter and immaterial force. This is the theory or declaration of faith of Christism. However, this theory may also have other older, classical forms. but Christism is more advanced, comprehensive. unified. and inclusive as it has been written and stipulated in the pages of this study. But whether the theory of Christism may have an impact upon or change how approach and live reality, it's much on the inspiration and motivation for the exposition of truth of the nature of God for the intents and purposes of human acknowledgment and recognition or identifying to/with his creator. Also, it offers relevance to the concept that every human perception of the nature of God at the present dispensation is at the mercy and modality of the pure act of faith; even given that faith has an absolute foundation of truth, the fact that we are still living in the mortal dimension of reality, the glorification of faith would only be received and confirmed when the immortal dimension will come. For this reason. Christism does offer a chance in the event that everything else would be a failure before God. This is an active act of faith regardless of the consequences because it's held as an absolute truth to oneself, not necessarily with regard that any other basis of faith is counterfeit but that faith must be based upon a reason to each proponent; otherwise, one would be committing a self-deception or doubt.

Truth will always be at the assertion of faith not only based upon philosophy or reason but also scientifically or materially on the sole basis that the actual nature of energy, its origin, and/or force couldn't possibly be completely explainable. Hence, absolute truth (by faith) is only attributable to time and space (immaterial things) relative to the fact that there would be no complete material relevance of truth. Not surprisingly, most proponents of materialism had consented to the nonexistence of God, perhaps on the basis that science couldn't find a direct relationship between electromagnetic and gravitational force but such relationship couldn't ever be found materially, regardless any form of force or energy or even matter itself is only a consideration of purpose so that all energy structures are only a transformation of the creator himself (God the father and God the son). But it's the space or nothing that to be considered the creator for the reason that it's the cause, origin.

and maintenance of all motion, energy preservation, and transformation. It's only on this basis that the nature of existence couldn't possibly be explainable. The demand of materialism to explain existence in terms of pure consistence of matter has failed because of the consideration of eternal motion and infinity. The very fact that science couldn't find a direct material relationship between electromagnetic and gravitational force should have been enough for science to understand that there's an immaterial creator that is in constant play with all physical existence that is created. bur rather (materialism) denied the existence of God. Science must accept the fact that it's only with the existence of the nothing (space) which has no energy field or material manifestation whatsoever but has a force that's cued in to all matter and creation, thereby holding the whole universal phenomena in space, then and only then would science believe the existence of God. Materialism will be forever lost from the truth of God, if it will continue to hold its concept, for the reason that the explanation of the issue of infinity couldn't possibly be explained in any material proposition. implied or direct.

Any considerations and speculations of truth must be confined to the argument of the purpose; for this reason, any attempt of immortality must begin and end with a purpose, and in this study of Christism, the purpose of God from the beginning and to the end (immortality) is physical or material existence. The Judeo-Christian perception of the nature of Christ has a limited relevance in terms of modem reality of historical events, but its general implication, if to be understood in a different perspective or point of view, very much has a veritable affinity of truth in this study (Christism), and such implication could even be far beyond what any rabbi or religious clergy could possibly imagine because such is the physical embodiment of the Cosmic Christ, even beyond the reach and scope of scientific speculations.

Whether we like it or not the sin of materialism is its own glory (become the creator of his own) and its rebellion against God—thus it sounds like Lucifer? Regardless, it's completely impossible for science to create an immortality of human existence as we know it. Humanity's best chance depends on the persistence of faith of the possibility of the existence of God regardless of adequate absurdities available with general existence. Universal physical existence existed out of mystical events, which science attributed as chance, while other schools of thoughts postulate that it's the act of God or with definite purpose. Both venture speculation about existence which gambles on the possibility of immortality on the same respective arguments that maybe some fortuitous event could lead science to the discovery of the ultimate secret of the universe and be able to tailor eternal life for humanity; on the other hand, religious practitioners remain adamant that such a mystery will offer complete redemption for humanity from all its dilemmas and problems.

For the sake of truth and the faith of God, therefore, any proposition, speculation, philosophy, religion, or theory of divine inspiration must be relevant upon its own merit and validity with respect to its affinity to the exposition, understanding, and acceptance of the mystery of existence to the personal opinion or perception of an individual to issue direct relationships of perception and divine inspiration because all adherence and reception of the truth will always have essence and value only with every individual choice and confirmation. Likewise, it must be of God who will judge solely according to the discretion/exercise of pure honesty of intent of every action and behavior. Absolute truth, therefore, could only derive real compromise or settlement between a believer direct relation with one's conviction/perception and his God. An individual's relationship to his government and fellow man must be secondary and auxiliary for the reason that evangelism must also pass through an individual perception and scrutiny for confirmation of personal faith. A violation of this schedule would be considered an insinuation of an attempt of the act of coercion. Individualism, therefore, must always be given priority in relation to the process of all attempts of the acquisition of truth. Because even if God leads one to the truth, the perception, determination, and confirmation must be solely a pure and unadulterated individual activity. This is the pure essence of the privilege of the authorization of liberty, which is completely sanctioned by God and is even stipulated in the Judeo-Christian Scripture in the book of Genesis when the first couple (Adam and Eve) were given the liberty to defect from the commandments and authority of their God. This is the justice and righteousness of a pure and holy God.

The evidence of truth is analogous to the presentation of freedom with direct relationship to the belief of the existence of God. The first and foremost socio-political supportive evidence is the very existence of the two greatest political or social management concepts: as socialism or communism and democratic or republican forms of government which respectively are given to the perception that there's no God and there's God.

Communism and socialism didn't recognize the fundamental principle of freedom as directly inseparable with the existence of perception. Perception couldn't proceed without freedom, similarly in physics that motion is impossible without space. If a communist could admit to himself that he had the ability of inherent perception, then he could only avoid the commission of the most grievous form of transgression of self-deception of believing of the existence of God or truth. Communism, therefore, is a system of belief that proliferated out of ignorance of the innate interrelationship of freedom and perception, and although it had the ability of experiencing the gift of perception, it lacks the real, most fundamental realization of the very nature of creation in general.

However, democratic forms of government themselves are not exempt or without blemish. The fact couldn't be denied that democratic governments themselves outrightly confused the suitable relationship of individual freedom and prohibition. For instance: without the existence of the freedom of prostitution, there couldn't be any possibility of an honest relationship between man and woman; neither could any sexual affairs of married or unmarried human beings possibly be philosophically unsuspected of coercion. The argument of "if" and/or if" must always be at consideration notwithstanding that the opposite of freedom is destruction or harm. This logic must preempt all the administration of prohibition. Any government which prohibits the exercise of prostitution has either undermined or missed the moral necessity as a balancing mechanism of the practice of it (prostitution) in human social (opposite sex, male to female) interactions because there's no morality with the absence of freedom or with the presence of coercion.

Religious Concepts, Christianity and Christism

The unified theory of universal existence, as it has been fully stipulated in this study, is the only viable resolution of the conflict of the demand of spiritual purpose and natural or physical law: that the embodiment of God is the whole universal physical reality—we called it creation; every atom and/or any form of accountable energy in it is the human assumed physical reality. Such embodiment is supported and/with eternal interaction with his creator—the nothing or space—in which makes it possible to be alive and possess a spirit. And since his creator is in constant interaction with its creation, the creator itself is able to retain its own life and spirit. The life-sustaining force of the universe, therefore, is eternal for the reason that the creator became completely nothing so that its interaction with its creation didn't require energy expenditure. Regardless, there are studies of physics or related sciences which have a proposition that energy could be destroyed to eternal oblivion. But such theorists could only deceive themselves for the reason that the origin of any form of energy hasn't been explained or found not to mention that man doesn't have the capability of universal space travel, and yet science is arrogant enough to claim that the universe's physical laws revolve solely with his understanding. This unilateral materialistic concept of existence could only be viable if human knowledge could find an answer to the most fundamental questions of where and how energy came about or originated. The Big Bang theory is not the origin of energy; it only stipulated the formation of the physical universe as man sees it, but not the origin of the rudimentary forms of energy. Besides, there might be more out there beyond the grasp of human perception or wisdom. The black hole theory stipulates the absence of energy, and it claims to consume energy because human intellect has only defined energy in terms of kinetic motion or force or potentials that human perception could recognize.

Mortality and all other forms of enigma or life's minor or major absurdities inflicted reason on human intellect which resulted in two major perceptions: science and religion, or the notion that there is no God or there is God. In this study of Christism, mortality and all absurdities of life, whether genetic or any natural phenomenon, have been reconciled as an inseparable structure or composition of the dilemma of integral purpose of creation: that any immortal dimension (that is to come) is not reversible phenomena; it's a once-and-for-all occasion—regardless that is consists of a period of mortality (a cutoff), as stipulated in this study. Such an immortal dimension (or even the existence of God) must precede a mortal dimension as a mechanism of recognition and/or appreciation.

The most fundamental aspect behind why science rejected God is perhaps its failure to recognize the existence of a complete immaterial force called space, nothing, or void. It's elusive as the connection between EMF and gravitation; Albert Einstein himself hadn't found and declared that gravitational force is not really a force in terms of material reality (but Einstein didn't recognize the truth in spite of the fact that he almost declared it). Regardless, it's so obvious that without such an element of existence there's no other way to explain why physical (cosmic or universal) existence exists. If science committed a grievous act of self-deception, perhaps it's only on the basis that he couldn't reconcile the presence of mortality. But as long as science looks in only one direction, that of searching the secret of physical existence he never finds it because in any stretch of logic or philosophy, any matter could only exist if there's a nothing or immaterial counterpart. Science couldn't accept the existence of a complete immaterial force for the reason that it brings about the acceptance of a spiritual creator or God the father. To a materialist. it would never be easy to accept that there's a God on the basis that it will completely change one's perception and reality or way of life; for instance, that an honest—only the honest—believer of God couldn't possibly avoid being compassionate. However even those who don't believe in God couldn't eradicate compassion completely as long as one lives its natural nature. God is not stupid; he wouldn't crate without generally implanting moral restraint (check and balance) especially with the most precious creation like human beings. This has been argued in Judeo-Christian Scripture with Apostle Paul who stipulated that man is saved by faith and not by works; however, St. James haggled that faith without works is dead.

Let it be illustrated that perhaps the most remarkable central message of all time regard to innate human nature as seen by the Judeo-Christian faith is in the Old Testament of the biblical life and times of the chosen people of God as the Israelites. The affair of God and the nation of Israel was centered in what was called the sanctuary which was prevalent from Genesis to Revelation. In the modern time, Christianity the sanctuary became the Church: a place of worship but its function is modified because of the Gospel—the free grace— but the primary objective hasn't been nullified as the Church remains a place of worship and a means of salvation. But before the crucifixion, the sanctuary was a sacred structure with two major parts: the Holy place and the most Holy place.

Actually, the concept of the tabernacle or sacrificial offering commenced after the fall of Adam and Eve such that Cain committed the first act of homicide by killing his brother Abel out of jealousy as to why God had blessed Abel's sacrifice while his was rejected. But the initial formal building of the sanctuary by the nation of Israel was conceived of God's direction through Moses in Exodus Chapter 25 of the Christian Scripture.

The purpose of the sanctuary is for the atonement of sins committed. And sin, whatever its attributes or origin, is an affair of transgression of the law whether natural or spiritual. "Thou shall not kill" is not only a religious—Jewish or Christian—law but also a natural law, one that is innate in human beings as given by God as stipulated in the structure of morality (see Structure of Morality). Because the nation of Israel during the Old Testament is actually a theocratic form of government so that all sin was a direct transgression of God's law, the recognition between the innate righteousness and the righteousness of the observance of all the commandments of God wasn't discernible without the sanctuary. Regardless, the sanctuary itself might have played a vital role in their economy, but the main objective of the sanctuary must be the instruction for the revelation of the nature of man with respect to his creator at that time.

The amenities in the tabernacle of the congregation and the most holy place have no relevance except that the overall significance of the sanctuary is nothing but sin and its reconciliation and salvation. Through simple deduction, that the sanctuary itself levied a form of taxation. The sanctuary installed guilt and healing of the human spirit or consciousness. The sanctuary, therefore, is a theology based upon the concept that man is naturally righteous, and that sin is the result of the transgression of God's laws and the only means of salvation is for an atonement to be made and carried out by the high priest for all in the most holy place. But the transfer or repentance of sin with offering must be an individual (people) act in the tabernacle of the congregation. The two phases of righteousness are apparent: one was transgressed, and the other is given back through the atonement. So, the sanctuary was divided into two compartments. The significance of the holy place is where the initial response of an individual who has recognized transgression and the willingness for reconciliation; such action is supported by material offerings. This action itself is already considered as righteousness not only by the offering but also because the initiation of the spirit of repentance was an act of God inside the individual; therefore, when the individual's perception has chosen repentance, he didn't offer resistance to the stimulus. The significance of the most holy place is the blessing of forgiveness or reconciliation for the restoration of the necessary righteousness for salvation; which is also conducted with an offering carried out by the high priest for all.

Biblical salvation as portrayed in the New Testament, although it fulfilled the purpose of the sanctuary, at the same time abolished it. Aaron, the high priest in the Old Testament, was just a symbolic representation of what is to come later through Christ the savior in the New Testament. Although it wasn't clearly understood why, the high priest himself became the sacrificial offering in the New Testament. The only technical explanation could be the fact that Jesus Christ was both a man and God incarnate, so that he could be the mediator (high priest) and the lamb of God at the same time, which, in turn, begat the concept that God reconciled man unto himself. In the New Testament, the main topic is the relationship of righteousness by faith and righteousness by work or law. Apostle Paul's letter to the Romans was very clear that only the righteousness by faith could merit salvation. This discourse is identical with the Old Testament's ceremonial proceedings. All the works, offerings, sacrifices in the holy place are the righteousness of the law or righteousness by works for the reason that the repentant sinner admitted his sins and guilt, thereby offering sacrifice for the hope of forgiveness. This is the act of the spirit of God and man at the same time. While in the most holy place, the repentant sinner is not allowed to enter but is completely represented by the high priest for the atonement of his sins. This is the work of a mediator or a Messiah (savior). This is the righteousness by faith. In the New Testament, the righteousness by faith is the work—life and death—of the savior Jesus Christ imputed to the believer or sinner.

There's an interesting similarity with regard to the sanctuary with the life and times of the chosen people of God: Israel. In the Old Testament the major observance of the sanctuary started after the nation (people) of Israel gained liberation from the Egyptian rule and were wandering in the desert without a native land. In the New Testament, the adjournment of the ceremonial observance of the sanctuary is reflected though the phrase *it's finished." Perhaps the dilemma to be attributed to the fact that Israel couldn't possibly liberate itself from the Roman empire, so the Romans contributed to the crucifixion or death of Christ. However, the Jewish nation shouldered the blame exonerated the Romans. It was the reason Pontius Pilate washed his hands.

The Christ event was quite interesting to observe by the logic that Israel probably would really like to try the separation of church and state—the free grace era of mentality. The only way to do this was to do away with the sanctuary, regardless of its necessity not only for the economy but for the truth. The climate of time--knowledge--was probably changing fast ("knowledge will increase"); a biblical prophecy was an indication that increase of knowledge was inevitable and might already started in their time However, hope and salvation didn't end with the dissolution of the sanctuary but the beginning of its fulfillment with the death of Christ and the extension of faith and hope in his second coming. The sanctuary, therefore, went to heavenly places (Revelation 11:19; 13:6) where it could never be endangered by human enemies. In fact. when the sanctuary was taken away from Earth, the direct communication between God and man was taken away. In fact, Jesus Christ himself said "When I'll be lifted up...I'll send you another comforter" which is the Holy Spirit.

The argument about the future of what would become of the Christian faith started heavily with Apostle Paul and St. James. The Pauline message liberalized the salvation by his concept of free grace (Romans 3:24) and that salvation is no longer only for the Jews but also for the Gentiles (Romans 3:29). Apostle Paul provided the mechanism for the unlimited evangelism of the truth. In fact, his message of justification by faith could be interpreted to be truthful in all manners or concepts of a belief in God. He understood that any form of morality or righteousness is worthless without faith in God (see also Structure of Morality), and such a genuine faith must bring forth good works. He was not very concerned about the law or work, but his admonition of righteousness was under the law of faith. Unlike St. James, who disputed faith, perhaps either that he didn't understand the full meaning of faith or was just being conservative of the keeping of the law for righteousness, entangled himself in the relationship of the law and the Gospel. In James 2:18-26, St. James had committed an anti-Gospel mentality by neglecting the very fact that it's impossible to separate honest faith and good works. The tendency of Apostle James to interchange faith with works (James 2: 18) is a valid erroneous view or understanding of the message of justification by faith, for Apostle Paul declared that the Gospel is the end of the law.

The sanctuary is the heart and soul of the Bible. In the New Testament and henceforth, the meaning of the sanctuary wasn't abolished; only the ceremonial laws were completely revoked. The sanctuary then transmogrified into Christian faith of various forms worshiped under the shelter of the structure of churches. The concept of Apostle Paul seemed to gain much more popularity with his proposition of free grace (Romans 3:24-28), meaning that salvation is not to be earned by any form of offering anymore or by any good works or fulfillment of the moral or ceremonial law but solely by faith in Jesus Christ.

It seemed that Apostle Paul was careless, but not when he recognized that everyone was a sinner (Romans 5:17-19; Romans 3:10-23) through the sin of Adam. Regardless that all have received the atonement through the righteousness by faith in Christ imputed for the believer, the problem of sin is not completely done, meaning that the capability to commit sin and transgression remains available. The sacrifice of Jesus didn't do away with the genetic propensity to commit sin but has provided a security of forgiveness and the coming salvation which will end the physical component of sin.

Apostle Paul wrestled with this problem in Romans 8:4-8. In his arguments he clearly understood the persistence of sin—which he himself experienced in Romans 7:14-25, which he blamed on the flesh. Apostle Paul, therefore, avoided confronting the dilemma of human nature by attributing the law and the Gospel as fully spiritual (Romans 7:14; 8:7). In biblical philosophy there's not enough room to settle the problem of human nature—fallen or otherwise—because of the nature of Christ or God or creation, according to the biblical foundation and the blueprints parameters of truth.

But whether the Christ event took place or not, the truth was communicated: there was a creation event that took place at some point in time with a purpose of a creator popularly known as God. And is this study (Christism) its best probability has been presented. Therefore, every representation which leads to the honest intent of such a worship—of any form—to the creator could be accepted for salvation or confirmation of the truth. Some cultures even worship the sun, volcano, etc. as God, but so be it, as long as the intent is honest for the concept of existence of God. Because the channel through which God communicates the truth is human perception, its manifestation is diverse because of the element of freedom and the unique individual inherent capacity. The more convenient mechanism for the understanding of the truth was by way of ceremonial activity relevant to the fact that it doesn't require high intellectual capacity for its acceptance; also, it utilizes the grace and justice of such a creator that salvation could be available to whoever will. Matthew 11:28-30: "…my yoke is easy and my burden is light." The Judeo-Christian Scripture of its sanctuary ceremonial conveyance of the truth was based on its profound philosophy but is simple enough to be observed and accepted by the ordinary or common follower. Although, there are numerous forms of simple religious practices that had been cultivated and proliferated, the Judeo-Christian faith is by far the most interesting and popular because of its simplicity and complexity which could indulge both the intellectual as well as the common man. In fact, the

Bible itself accepted the very essence of the truth hat God is no respecter of persons (Romans 2:11) and also further issued validity to the idea that everyone is equal before God. But it doesn't matter form of worship is employed to exhibit one's personal belief to a creator. The Bible also admitted that even under a tree one could worship God because what matters is the honest intent of such worship or dedication of such activity for the acknowledgment of the existence of God (Romans 10:13). Any activity honestly and profoundly dedicated to God must be acceptable to God, even giving alms to the poor with the intent that such an act of charity is based on the concept that God is love is by itself an act of worship. Any act of goodness with respect to a faith in God could merit salvation. Apostle Paul argued.

The Judeo-Christian faith, although it may or may not be the most practiced religion on planet Earth at the present time, is the most sensible and practical approach of the truth--of the existence of God—in the form of religion. For anybody who would like to extract the truth of the Bible, it must be accomplished by way of careful analysis of the meaning (philosophical) of the ceremonial activities of the Old Testament tabernacle and sanctuary and the gospel of the New Testament. Even if the Bible is a fictional work of literature or an actual historical event, it doesn't change the meaning and purpose Or existence of the truth. However, the biblical truth must not be imposed upon anybody; otherwise, it will destroy itself of its truth and/or purpose. This Study of Chrisrism concerns all forms of religion with similar intentions of the exercise or understanding of the truth of the existence of God, so that the Judeo-Christian faith is not any different than a group of individuals who honestly worship the sun, rat, or what have they for the sole, honest intent of understanding the existence of God. Absolute truth is an individual perception, as stipulated in this study, regardless of any or with any divine inspiration, because God never coerces nor is the language of God of any man but by his spirit which communicates through human nature as he himself created all existence in his own will. Even the Christian faith must be understood—in the mind/perceived—either ceremonially or intellectually before it could be viably accepted or practiced by any individual. The practice and utility of any religion must be universal. Apostle Paul's concept of free grace is the most profound understanding of such a spirit or will of God; otherwise, it violates the very nature of God. Apostle Paul might have understood the problem of the Old Testament, that God was limited for the Jews or Israel alone (Romans 3:29, also John 3:16); God must not be a racist. Likewise, any form of religion outside the Judeo-Christian faith must submit itself to this concept of universal free grace; otherwise, it's irrational.

All religious belief has a physical identity or embodiment of its faith in God. In Christian religion, God is represented with the image of Jesus Christ ("the word became flesh") who is in the form of a human being (Genesis 1:27). Other religions might have the sun, volcano, rat, cow, or anything under the sun or above which could be regarded as God. In this study of Christism, these religious (Christ, sun, volcano, etc.) methodologies are regarded as a separatist concept of the nature of God, not only that all religious belief has a physical identity or substance of God but also that such a god must be powerful. The definition of the power of the gods varies from one religion to another. And beside the power of the gods, such a god must be capable of salvation for the immortality of the believer. The concepts of salvation and immortality also diverge from one religion to another. All forms of religion, therefore, have a concept of truth, and if the truth is established in such a fashion that it becomes "the only truth." It would result in the fragmentation of society and often lead discrimination and violence in sectarian rivalry. Christism is a study that relates itself to the concept of the Universalist Pauline Gospel: that a free salvation is available to everyone who believes in God (Romans 3:24-28). The Judeo-Christian concept of a divine being, like all its separatist counterparts, could find itself (themselves) with a dilemma of probing or effectuating physical and or material evidence of the power and mysticism of their gods. The Christ of the Christians who went to heavenly places had completely abandoned his earthly followers, and such a promise of a second coming could be seen as a panacea or philosophical necessity of its writers or proponents. This is not to challenge the gods, but the demand of reason and truth must be accomplished. In this study of Christism, it has been stipulated and confirmed the most reasonable probability of the existence of God which had the embodiment of the whole universal physical reality, or the Cosmic Christ, which also has the capacity of salvation and immortality not only for himself but also for all universal existence. It's only in this fashion of the embodiment of God that the claim of all religions could be made manifest. The Jesus Christ concept of the Judeo-Christian faith could be theologically integrated with the Cosmic Christ without altering major religious ceremonialism and formalism practices. Because all religion is a belief in God (theology) systems, the mechanism of theological integration of upgrading of all religion with the Cosmic Christ is very simple, and it doesn't require many changes of any practices of faith: for example, the cultural practice of the belief that the sun or volcano is a god. All it takes to harmonize or integrate this belief system with the Cosmic Christ is to incorporate one's faith that the sun or volcano is just a part of a greater Cosmic God which is greater reality with all the mysteries of nature or existence.

Even the Jesus of the Christian faith who is believed to be God's incarnate ("the word became flesh") had worshiped a heavenly father when he was on Earth. Although, Jesus Christ claimed that he was one with the father, he only meant in purpose, not in physical reality in terms of the Christians perception of truth or creation, but in Christism (the unified theory of existence) everything/everyone in one with God the father.

In the Judeo-Christian Scripture there wasn't a disclosure of the nature of God the Father. So, even if the Jesus Christ event of the Bible was a real historical account, Jesus himself has a father who is in heaven, and the only insinuation provided in the Bible as to the nature of God the Father is a spirit. The only way such a spirit could make a revelation is through mysterious manifestations, as has been revealed with the Old and New Testaments with his chosen nation, Israel. Even Moses couldn't have been much more a believer and a deliverer without seeing and having utilized (God's) mysterious circumstances. But even with mysterious (biblical) occurrences of such a magnitude the fate of humanity's mortality remains intact and unchanged. Even if the Christ event is true, he is also a creature of God the father. The Bible itself acknowledged that the spirit or word in the Old Testament became Christ. So, who's the father in in heaven referred to by Jesus who's on Earth? It couldn't be that Jesus was praying and talking out loud to himself? If (one is) to seek God's revelation in the present time is reproachable, then at least the period or dispensation of the message of justification by faith (it's only in the New Testament that Abraham's works were counted for righteousness by faith [Romans 4:2, 16) must be reconciled with the diametrical nature of times between the biblical and the present, such that faith has completely done away with the mysterious acts of God? And if the Israelites had even doubted Moses in his time, despite the magnitude of mysteries during their time, people living in the present time are probably better followers or believers than the previous (Israel) chosen people of God. Whether like it or not, any serious scrutiny of biblical events (or meaning of events) still requires, if not a lot, philosophical exegesis to determine the direction of interpretation for more approachable logical validity, or just to satisfy the demand of reason and/or doubt, because at the same time the eventual occurrence (timing) of the message of justification by faith (Gospel) and the complete disappearance of actual mysterious events. If doubt is certain of the validity whether biblical claims are faithful or not, the theory of Christism could be vital (for validity) as a recourse or resource of faith or a new faith.

The Urgency of Embracing, Integration, and/or Religious Upgrade to the Cosmic Christ According to Christism

All forms of religious faith or belief systems could embrace or be integrated with or upgraded to the concept of Christism without the peril or risk of losing of one's prospect of salvation. For instance, in the Christian faith either Protestantism or Catholicism, as the most sophisticated form of religion on planet Earth today, could embrace the concept or message of Christism while at the same time completely retaining most of its forms and belief system.

Whether religions would like it or not, knowledge will continue to ascend or increase not decrease; this is the nature of creation of the evolutionary act of God. And any religious organization which is deliberately or willfully engaged in activity or operation to suppress or subdue in any manner, shape, or form the ascent of human scrutiny in all aspects of religion, literature, philosophy or reason, or even scientific knowledge and preach a faith that God is righteous and just, doesn't only commit outright hypocrisy but also proclaims its disbelief in God, and only interest in the commerce of religion lurks with the pretext of moralistic garb or superficial intentions. However, if all religions are honest, then all religions must allow into themselves scrutiny and the dissemination of all other religious or philosophical beliefs to the general public, because if there is such a God, such a God must allow the complete exercise of freedom—so much so that any individual who's honest and moral in the execution of freedom must exactly know by nature that harm and greed have no part whatsoever with the practice of personal liberty or the dissemination of it.

The progressive ascent of knowledge or perception must be a direct or indirect purpose of our creator. And such a creator or God couldn't possibly be worried about how much scientific or other knowledge a human being could acquire because gods are indestructible both physically and philosophically and the ultimate understanding of the nature of universal or local existence couldn't possibly be found. Just one instance of this is the consideration of infinity. As a matter of fact, the study and pursuit of physical science always lags behind the advancement of philosophy or theoretical speculations; thereby only philosophy could possibly offer a better understanding of the very nature of God because of the physical limitations of scientific achievement. And because the ultimate technical approach or methodology of any concept of immortality couldn't possibly be achieved by any creature but a creator, philosophy or reason or spiritual inspiration are the only mediums by which a creature could possibly engage in the prospect of the understanding of eternal existence of or the nature of God. The purpose of any proposition of eternity (God) must be dealt with; accordingly, otherwise, eternity is but an empty idealism. As has been stipulated previously in this study, God's purpose is physical existence, not only for humanity but also for God himself, and such a concept has been inspired that all religious beliefs—since the beginning of time—do worship a God with physical embodiment or manifestation.

The scope of philosophy or reason or spiritual understanding not only requires the theoretical management of truth (absolute if possible) but also its physical dynamics or its physical embodiments and/or utility. Any religious belief or system must therefore be willing to accommodate a philosophical/physical scrutiny of its truth to afford itself of the capabilities of its God; otherwise, a religion could retreat into a shell because its God is very sensitive and vulnerable to reason. If religion would choose to be invulnerable, then it must embrace a theoretical management of truth such that it must be willing to participate in all propositions of the possibilities of probabilities of the logic of: *if, even if,* then (even God must have answered the questions of probabilities before he created anything), because not only that physical science is poised with universal quest of space travel and understanding, but it's also that it seemed that all religious beliefs are earthly and institutionalized and that all earthly religion could be vulnerable to earthly racism in universal terms. A very similar concept was embraced by Apostle Paul in Romans 3:24-28 when he saw that God is not only for the Jews but also for the Gentiles, by which the term *Gentiles* could be applied universally. But even if science would not be able to conclude that there are other life forms in other parts of this very huge span of physical reality and universal existence, could philosophy or reason avoid the issue of all possibilities? Did the God of the Judeo-Christian faith land on Earth because it's the only planet possible for a life form? And would such a God deny humanity the truth of it? And if that God returned to heaven after he created humanity in his own image and likeness, what could the nature of existence in heavenly places be?

Unlike other religions—like those who worship the sun, volcano, cow, rats, or what have they—most obviously must reconcile or embrace or even integrate or just upgrade to the theory of Christism for the simple fact that not only are they easily vulnerable to even just elementary scrutiny of reason, but also it couldn't possibly stand the least judgment of universal proposition of truth. However, when such rudimentary forms of religion would upgrade themselves to the truth of Christism, these religious or cultural faiths could also acquire durability or resistance from intense scrutiny of reason.

The Christian faith is perhaps the most interesting form of religion to be upgraded or to embrace the theory of Christism primarily by its sophisticated knowledge and extensive appeal of morality; however, it doesn't seem completely invulnerable to scrutiny of reason, regardless that it seemed to provide itself covert philosophical shields against heavy criticism by way of anticipation through systematic chronological expositions of its doctrines. It's also the duty of this study to provide the mechanism by which the greatest religious form on Earth (Christianity) be able to embrace or integrate/upgrade itself to the theory of Christism primarily for the sake of its survival.

Apostle Paul had lived during the period of inevitable separation of ideology in his time (Corinthians 1:23) and also the increase of knowledge (Corinthians 1:22). The law and the Gospel concept of salvation demanded distinctive arguments as to what the future of the concept not only of the existence of God would be evangelized but also of the nature of the management of society would be. The law, as the most expert mechanism for the management of society, has taken course with the concept of salvation by works by which St. or Apostle James had advanced in his stipulation in his book James 2:18-20. This speculation of St. James made him an advocate of anti-Gospel rationality, and it doesn't matter whether he understood the meaning of faith or the Gospel or not, because his error is so obvious. Apostle James conservatively contended that obedience of the law has a valid contribution or participation for salvation by expostulating that work is also faith (James 2:18). Apostle James didn't understand that in the period or era of the dispensation of the Gospel (grace), all human righteousness or obedience to the law must be clearly and absolute defined as a work of man (righteousness of the obedience of the law of man for man) and faith is faith as the righteousness of God (fulfilling all the demands of the law) for (imputed) man. Regardless of the fact that Apostle James understood that faith without work is dead, it doesn't justify his error for the reason that Apostle Paul also advocated the same principle that fait must work.

At the utmost stretch of philosophy, St. James would be regarded as a religious materialist, a legalist. He may or may not have consciously know it, but his ignorance and/or carelessness is manifested in that he had committed that most grievous mistake of his ministry because even at the present time, some religious Christian sects still adhere to his principle. Probably the appeal of the law is of its coercive nature for the management/acquisition of morality and its great ease of capability for the stabilization of civilization. However, it inherently possesses a very unfavorable and unsophisticated backlash from another aspect of argument for a better way for the exercise of morality. From the perspective of conscience and faith, morality or righteousness could be available and serviceable even without the law (Romans 1:20, Romans 7:9, Romans 4:15, Romans 7:8). But because, according to the biblical chronology of events, the prominence of law as the manager of morality, good and evil, or righteousness was established before the Gospel (Romans 1:31), in this regard, it could remain even under the dispensation of grace, but its

115

role must remain and well defined as it is: that it has no participation or merit whatsoever for salvation (Romans 1:17; Romans 1:28; Romans 4:2, 16). The coming of justification by faith means that the understanding of the existence of God became absolute so that even if all the law would be put away righteousness would abound (Romans 7:4, 7:9); after all, in the book of Genesis, in the Garden of Eden, there were no laws but one. (The fall of Adam could be related to the general inference in all manners of the quest of truth that sometime and somewhere in the distant past there must be an origin of all the absurdity of living or what is sociologically and religiously or generally referred to as "sin," and the interpretation and its ramification could vary from various perspectives and perceptions, but in the study of Christism the structure of morality is provided as a general guide for consideration because all perception of truth is individual regardless that it could be influenced in a lot of ways, but honesty must be the overriding principle if such a God does exist.)

The argument of Apostle Paul is vividly or distinctly well written in his Epistles to the Romans, even to a complete stranger to Judeo-Christian theology. Apostle Paul's argument of justification (salvation) by faith is quite simple, that salvation or righteousness that could only merit salvation is not, never was, and never will be an act of man. The meaning and object of faith must always be outside of the believer, something man can't manipulate or change for his own subjective purposes: otherwise, it's not faith. However, the response of faith (inspired by the very spirit of God) within a believer must be dynamic, otherwise, that faith is dead or false or counterfeit because there's no thing as an evil God. God must always be righteous and just.

Although Apostle Paul is the greatest amongst the apostles by contributing most of the books in the New Testament of the Bible, he didn't understand human nature. However, he is a man of faith, but he has the tendency to advocate Spiritualism (Romans 8:2-15). Regardless, Apostle Paul's contribution of the concept of justification by faith must remain the predominant aspect of his ministry. It's obvious that Apostle

Paul wrestled with the relationship of sinful human nature which prevails regardless of the law and the Gospel (Romans 7:14-17; Romans 8:6-16), but the Gospel took precedence as the power unto salvation.

The power of faith is unmatched for its capability of honesty, integrity, sincerity, etc., which the law couldn't do. Faith doesn't necessarily require law or vice versa, because faith has an inherent law of its own, "the law of faith." (Romans 1:27; see Romans 14:19-23). The exhortation of Apostle Paul through the Gospel even transcends the requirements of the given law. Abiding in faith on the whole Gospel message could produce a morality which the law couldn't possibly do. The downside of the law is that it has no mechanism or ability to render or produce morality or obedience with complete willingness or freedom. The alternative of faith (Romans 10:4) doesn't actually do away with the laws of government (Romans 1:31) but supplies its deficiency and curbs its oppression (Romans 4:15). Without the Gospel as the message of righteousness and salvation, humanity wouldn't have the most effective mechanism for the utilization of forgiveness and humility which is a necessity of the survival of civilization not only between individuals but between individuals and their government or ruler. The Gospel or the message of justification by faith actually served as the mechanism for the destruction of the theocratic form of government in which an institution where the belief of God is mandated by law of society or government. In any rational belief in the existence of God, the idea that God never coerces must be the overriding principle for the validity of justice of such a faith or religious concept. Any government couldn't possibly enforce religion or faith because of the incapability of the law to determine the measure of honesty and sincerity of intent which is a strict and absolute demand of the justice and righteousness of (a rational belief in the existence of God) God. A fundamentalist government which doesn't separate the power of church and state is an outright enemy of the belief of the existence of God. This is an outright act of hypocrisy in the biggest stretch of philosophical understanding of the existence of such a God. Apostle Paul's declaration of faith that Christ (Gospel) is the end of the law issued validity for the separation of church and state.

In the synoptic gospel of the life and times of Christ, the apparent enemies of the message of Jesus Christ were the scribes and Pharisees. These are the groups of people who were suspicious of the activity of the Messiah; they were looking for every little breach of the law to incriminate Jesus for the purpose of preserving the status quo to which they belonged, until finally the Jews crucified Christ. So, the law killed God. In the synoptic gospel of Matthew, Mark, Luke, and John, the transition of the message of the conflict of the relationship of the law and Gospel were already well defined for the destruction of the sanctuary and the law as the medium of salvation (John 3:16). St. James was the last advocate of that struggle in favor of legalism or salvation by the law of work, and Apostle Paul was the greatest defender of the Gospel or the message of justification by faith. In his epistle to the Corinthians, Apostle Paul (1 Corinthians 1:23) depicted the position of the message of the Gospel: "But we preach Christ crucified, unto the Jews a stumbling block, unto the Greek foolishness."

The struggle of the law against the Gospel didn't end with St. James and Apostle Paul; it extended even into the fourteenth and the sixteenth centuries by which Martin Luther championed the message of justification by faith that leads to the conception of the religion of Protestantism. The struggle was representative of the law against the Gospel: the demise of the Roman Empire; the blessing of individual rights that came about during the period of the Middle Ages of the reign of the Barbarians; the translation of the Bible into the English language and the individual right to be able to read and interpret the scriptures advocate by John Wycliff; and the reformation revolution, which was the rebirth of the message of the Gospel—the justification by faith—advocated by the reformer Martin Luther in the sixteenth century or early fifteen hundred.

Although, Protestantism is not a complete reform movement from Catholicism because some, if not all, Protestant sects embrace the concept of Baptism and the Eucharist, the message of the Gospel or justification by faith has regained its presence. The problem of both Protestantism and Catholicism with regard to the concept of the Apostle Paul on the Gospel, is the confusion that faith has to be justified with works. The huge discrepancy of the concept of absolute or pure faith with that tainted faith with any works of man must be relevant mostly to financial obligations—under the names or tithes and offerings and other civic obligations. The mentality and rationale of legalists or the concept of St. James in his assertion of the requirement that faith must be justified by work is an anti-Gospel according to Apostle Paul. Faith doesn't have to be asked what it could do because it violates the principle of the integrity of faith itself, as well as the justice and righteousness of God. It's a blasphemy in the concept of the free grace and mercy of God because God's love is unconditional so that even while we were yet sinners, according to Apostle Paul, Christ died for us. It's pathetic indeed that the straightforward righteousness of God imputed for sinners that has been presented by Apostle Paul very clearly has continued to be misunderstood—probably deliberately for some reason for the sake of economic benefit and the structure of hierarchy or status quo. But morally there's nothing more honest and virtuous or pure than the concept of justification by faith through the Gospel of Jesus Christ.

It's legal or appropriate to solicit tithes and offerings or any act of civic obligation from believers but not in the name of salvation, not anymore, according to the Gospel; otherwise, we would like to crucify God again. The Gospel has already done away with all the ceremonial requisites of the sanctuary as well as all the demands of the law. This is the object of faith which, in human terms will embrace the law but not anymore for salvation but as a result of the hope of salvation, and in the Gospel's (God's) terms. God died for the law for the justification of all sins but not to reconcile God to man but man to God, because there's no human righteousness that could merit salvation. Faith supplied the deficiency of the law, and the law will not supply any deficiency of faith.

In any stretch of the law couldn't measure the intent of righteousness which is supposedly honest and sincere; it's only through faith that the intent of righteousness of a believer could be measured by God. To measure the intent of faith through the amount of works is enmity to the principle of the nature of God: that God never directly or indirectly coerces for the very reason that salvation is free. This is the direct contrast of the Old and New Testaments of biblical philosophy. Regardless that man became the temple of God (1 Corinthians 3:16), most religions of the present time still haven't really changed from the Old Testament philosophy for the very reason that the interpretation of biblical theology hasn't been embraced in philosophical terms for general existence but is limited to the interpretation of symbolic to actual events, for example, the sanctuary which symbolized the coming of the Messiah but not as also with profound significance of human nature's overall existence.

The general task of the Gospel is actually freedom with honesty, integrity, and sincerity. In all forms of government, socialism or democratic, the power of the law is always employed as the only viable mechanism of compliance. In socialism and communism where God isn't perceived, the law is utilized solely to afford material equality or the equal distribution of wealth. In democratic forms of government where God is perceived, the law is employed to prevent chaos of the process of competition of wealth. But in either situation, as in any form of government, the law will always have its deficiency for the management of human existence whether morally, materially, or in any avenue of human life, but the most immediate casualty in any form of human management is freedom. And the lesser the freedom the more we restrict the communication between God and man, and the exercise of faith is threatened. It's only with the extent of the availability of freedom that God is able to measure the properties of faith. So, in a government like socialism by which faith in God is not available, salvation is also not available because it couldn't be possibly processed. Even if the Spirit of God is in all human beings, if response is not made through faith, then salvation couldn't be available.

Regardless that communism and socialism are capable of establishing righteousness between man to man; the righteousness between man to God which is of faith alone is not available. So, for the legalist or any who advocate that any act of righteousness that is done with regard to any law religious or government could merit salvation is a huge, obvious mistake. This is what is referred to by Apostle Paul as the righteousness of the law in the book of Romans 10:4-13 which contrasts the definition of work and faith.

Any act of righteousness, be it of the obedience of law of government or religion, if it's rendered for the law couldn't merit salvation. However, any act of righteousness (be it of the obedience of any law) which is intended for God then it's a result of faith. The natural man who hasn't heard of God is capable of righteousness which is considered as the exemption of faith and such judgment is solely of God's own discretion. Faith, therefore, is nota material act but a spiritual acknowledgment of the existence of God, and such perception results in the performance of virtue and obedience of the law. This aspect of faith has been understood by Apostle Paul in Romans 10:3-16. Faith is a freedom from the law. The Gospel has divorced man from the law (Romans 7:4,6). The motive of why salvation is by faith is itself the nature of God or truth which is fair, just, and holy, and such a nature of God couldn't possibly be depicted by any obedience of the law for the sole reason that law is coercive in nature at all times and in all situations. Biblical reality, therefore, faith, in the New Testament has retroactively redeemed man even from Abraham (Romans 4:1-5), not only in religious reasoning but also in the real world of philosophical existence whenever man is not restricted of reason, unlike in socialist and communist governments in which the philosophy mostly focuses on material existence.

In real life situations of individuals, whether in a religious or socio-political setup and whether the relationship is hostile or amiable situation, the law and the Gospel (faith) is always dynamic. The dynamics of faith tend to oppose the law, but when it obeys, it enhances the law. The dynamics of the law tends to suppress faith (freedom), but when it slackens, faith is glorified. Just one popular profound example of this argument is the prohibition of prostitution. Whenever there's a law prohibiting the clean and honest exercise of prostitution, all sexual relationships between man and a woman are practically an act of coercion. To bypass the philosophical requirement of this concept and pretend that is has no bearing with the concept of the existence of God is a complete mediocrity and anathema to the very nature of God. Even the Christ of the Bible encountered the same dilemma with the scribes and Pharisees (legalist) in his life and times depicted in the Bible by the synoptic gospels

If we look a little deeper even in modem times, at how the spirit of the Gospel has been trodden down by the spirit of legalism, in most if not all religious institutions, even the governments are involved in the destruction of even the very least fundamental individual right of students by imposing a mandatory school uniform just for the sake or purpose of material gain. They purport moral but what could be more moral than not treating the human mind as a circuit board for institutional moral experiments and letting the little children enjoy innocuous freedom of the Gospels. Even Jesus Christ clearly assailed the motive and intent of the scribes and Pharisees and issued a controversial statement that the harlots and publicans could go to the kingdom of God before them (Matthew 21:31).

If the message of the Gospel of Jesus Christ is only interpreted for its promise of salvation of immortal life, then such an interpretation could only lead to religious unilateral materialism. If the salvation of eternal life is the only motive and purpose of a believer in the obedience of the law and the intent of acquiring or having righteousness, then it's not any different than the righteousness of the scribes and Pharisees. The real message of the Gospel, or justification by faith according to Apostle Paul, hasn't been understood even to the present time.

To reiterate, the main thesis or assertion of the Gospel is freedom, by clearly alienating salvation from any obedience of the law (Rom. 7:4-6,

Rom. 11:6, Rom. 3:28). This is the only concept that could do away with the coercive nature of the law (Rom. 8:3-4). Christ died for the law; to explain fully how the insatiable demand of the law, the Gospel or the concept of justification by faith the most profound logic or philosophy of human existence is probably of all time. But if Christ didn't really exist, it could be the most misunderstood if not reconciled with the message of Christism, and the consequences could be very unfavorable. Whether we like it or not, if the Christ event didn't take place, the only possible salvation is to embrace the study of Christism.

The Gospel as we know it through the Bible is the reconciliation of man (sin) unto God or that God reconciled man unto himself. Why man needs to be reconciled to God is because of sin according to the law. The law brought all manners of sin and guilt into humanity. Without the law there's no sin (Romans 7:7-11). In Judeo-Christian theology the law existed before sin so that sin is the transgression of the law (read the book of Genesis). However, in the historical study of anthropology (outside religion) sin most probably existed before the law. But even if the condition of sin preexisted to warrant the establishment of the law, the law could never change its coercive nature. So, the argument of the Gospel is that the Savior or Messiah must die to fulfill all demands of the law for reconciliation because the law couldn't condemn with punishment and at the same time forgive.

The argument of reconciliation of the Messiah is a message that explained the dilemma of all times: that the existence of the law is always necessary until humanity could have an immortal life, so the coercive nature of laws is reconciled by the argument of faith and everlasting desire of freedom. The message of the Gospel then is centered as the message of forgiveness, reconciliation or salvation. The agony of the crucifixion must be a message with full relationship to the argument of freedom that any administration of the law must always consider.

Yet despite the sacrifice of Christ, the law completely neglected the event. More laws are legislated as harsher and more oppressive that ever and beyond what is necessary. The dilemma of prohibition against prostitution and the imposition of the school uniform is just a speck or an atom of the tip of the iceberg. The message of Christ is compassion, forgiveness, freedom from oppression, righteousness, etc. Salvation is not understood that it will be rewarded only upon those who believe in the person of Jesus Christ and not for those who work for the law to obtain righteousness for eternal life.

The archenemies of the biblical Christ are the legalists, the scribes and the Pharisees, the advocate of righteousness by works, and those who believe in God for the sake of eternal life. These are the religious materialists who believe that they could participate in the salvation for themselves and for humanity. The archenemies of the Cosmic Christ in the theory of Christism is Unilateral Materialism and Spiritualism. Although, there seems to be a tendency of Apostle Paul to be a spiritualist in the way he understood human nature, his remarkable presentation of the Gospel undermined his weakness, because the message of Christ is the heart and soul of the New Testament theology. The death and resurrection of the biblical Christ and the message of justification by faith represent a concept of the most approachable truth not only in philosophy/reason but also directly comparative to the concept of Christism that the Cosmic Christ would be solely responsible for the coming of the immortal dimension by which an operation beyond the capability of man, including all its sciences, because the unified energy structure of universal existence such that life on Earth fully depends upon the life and death of the sun in the solar system, and the sun itself is just a part of a huge universal phenomena. To expect human knowledge to be able to consider the whole universe or universes as his laboratory for human immortality, such a proposition of expectation, to reason and logic it is much easier to believe that the biblical Christ might have existed.

The simple fact is that the central message of Christian religion in its entirety is the Gospel or the justification by faith, regardless that most if not all of them have not clearly embraced or understood the real implication or simply avoided it for the reason of its controversial nature. The nature of the message of the Gospel or justification by faith is directly amenable to the theory of the Cosmic Christ, according to this study of Christism. The Gospel of the biblical Christ has brought the following shifts of theology in Judeo-Christian religion:

1. That salvation is taken away from the management of the sanctuary and the law.
2. That salvation is taken away from the management of any human hierarchy, power, or clergy.
3. That salvation is free to all those who believe in Jesus Christ as the savior.
4. That salvation is only a result or blessing of faith or belief in Christ. So that those who seek salvation would not find it, but those who believe in Christ will be rewarded of eternal life.

The concept of why Jesus Christ was born in a stable or from a poor family was probably supposed to elude the religious materialist, the scribes, and the Pharisees who were only looking for salvation. They had forgotten that Adam and Eve were immortal because they believed in God, and God issued one law to give them the consciousness of freedom of the existence of good and evil. Because immortality existed before the law in like manner, faith in God must exist before salvation, and such faith must only be obtained through freedom and not with any insinuation of coercion or obedience of the law. It was apparent that the constant conflict between Christ and the scribes and Pharisees over the law was that the message of Christ was diametrical to the existing prominent concept of salvation. It's obvious that the Old Testament theology of salvation is not only faulty and erroneous in terms of philosophical correctness but also in terms of the overall truth of the concept of the nature of the character of God of fairness and purity. And such a purity Of God could only be illustrated or communicated by the message of free grace or justification by faith. Any religious speculation of truth that doesn't comply with the truth of justification by faith is guilty of dogmatism, a theology of salvation by work or salvation by philosophy. Justification by faith is salvation by a belief to a person of Jesus Christ but not to a creed, theory, philosophy, or dogma.

The scribes and Pharisees were ardent religious materialists with their fervent desire and obedience to the law. When Jesus was born to a poor family instead of the anticipated palaces of a king, it might have been very disappointing to the scribes and Pharisees, for how could a savior born in a stable bring them salvation? The concept of salvation by one's works doesn't only apply to the Old Testament theology but also to any religious belief system that relies on salvation through the observation of a ceremonial system (with or without offerings and sacrifices) or dogma rather than a trust and faith in the person or embodiment of their God.

Without the message of justification by faith, humanity would be bound and destined to robotic moralism. Regardless of the presence of the concept of separation of church and state, the actual distinct separation of the legislation of laws couldn't possibly take place for the very fact that: 1) politicians have religious affiliations, 2) individuals or group of individuals that embrace religious dogma or belief couldn't possibly be prohibited the freedom of suffrage, 3) agnostics and atheists aren't any different from religious dogma or philosophy.

Until an individual will embrace the message of justification by faith (pure Gospel) there's no other possible way to have an open mind free from the entanglement of the fear that God wouldn't save you if you can't do this and that. It must be clearly understood that the message of justification by faith doesn't prohibit or prevent the obedience of the law—any law—but not for salvation. Obedience of the law is only a righteousness before or with fellow man, but not for salvation before God because God doesn't require, because God never coerces, because God is fair and pure and could read the intent of faith. God always knows that

126

honest faith will always do honest work, so for God to ask what faith must work or tell us what to do is needless. But of course, God must be always compromising the fact that he sees the intent more than perfectionism.

Any religion or an concept of the existence of God that relies on salvation alone in the strict observance of dogma or theory, is for the sole intent for salvation rather than to God, and if such a religious belief system believes that God requires offering and creed for salvation, then such religion or concept of God must be completely overhauled, because such a system of belief is completely untruthful to the proposition of the existence of God; such a system of beliefs is analogous to the Old Testament concept of God in the Judeo-Christian Bible, and such a belief system needs to be reconciled and embrace the concept of Christism for salvation.

Any religion or concept of the existence of God which performs or observes religious ceremonial activity or laws with the sole intent of making an offering to God, whether or not God in return reward salvation. then such a system of belief is reconciled to the truth because such a concept of a system is not for the concept but for God. This concept is relevant to the message or justification by faith because the intent of faith could only be evaluated by God alone for salvation. The contention of Apostle Paul was that faith will work for the reason that such an honest perception of the existence of God couldn't possibly afford to exhibit behavior that is contrary to the concept of the righteous nature of a divine being. The argument of faith promotes morality or righteousness that is completely unsolicited, but when solicited such responses aren't attributed the acquisition of salvation, because faith has already saved the believer before the action of any good works.

Faith itself is a perception or concept, and just like all the rest of the religious or scientific concepts, theories, or philosophical reasoning, it only warrants two probable bits of relevance to the pursuit of ultimate or absolute truth, to be: either unilateral materialism or of the existence of God. All forms of materialism, either scientific or religious, are conceptual of reality that ended or recoiled its ultimate truth or value unto itself. As in scientific unilateral materialism, which admitted the nonexistence of God, therefore, the truth is the concept itself—that the universe was created by chance and has no definitive purpose of its future destiny but to the final destruction of energy. With the case of religious materialists, the motive of its obedience and legislation of the law if focused on the basis of the reward of immortality by God. So that to a legalist such as the scribes and Pharisees, the concept of God is salvation, which is very evident when exposed in the synoptic gospel or the Old Testament theology of the Bible. But in the New Testament a sudden shift of theology has occurred: once and for all the theorists of the Bible have found a concrete philosophy of truth of the nature of the righteousness of God. The struggle of the message of the Gospel or justification by faith continued throughout the ages of history. One huge occasion, and probably the most recent since the crucifixion, was the battle of Dr. Martin Luther against Catholicism by which he (Martin Luther) protested the selling of indulgences. The concept of the selling of indulgences wasn't new; it was actually a rebirth of the Old Testament theology. But due to lack of faith of the existence of God, religious management couldn't do away with the concept of salvation by works for the sake of power, the management of morality and economic benefit.

All religious concepts that don't embrace the message of the Gospel or the concept of justification by faith fall into the pitfall of materialism. All religious concepts could embrace the message of the Gospel, and consequently, the theory of Christism. Even the religion that worshiped idols or anything under or above the sun could embrace the Gospel or justification by faith through and with the aid of the theory of Christism. Dr. Martin Luther himself recognized the significance of the justification by faith as the final and ultimate argument of truth that it determines the rise and fall of religious belief. And whether we like it or not, all religious concepts must be judged on the message of the Gospel or justification by faith for the sake of the ultimate argument of absolute truth for it's the pure righteousness of any concept of the existence of God. Even with the pure theory of Christism, justification by faith, even regardless of the biblical Christ (see Structure of Morality), it's the cause of salvation, and its effect is good works or righteousness. All religious concepts can embrace the theory of Christism without the knowledge of the biblical Christ or Gospel. But nobody could bypass the concept of justification by faith as long as God exists. Because faith is an individual (or group with the same objective) relationship of **acknowledgment** of the existence of the personhood or embodiment of the creator or God (in biblical theology this includes the life and death of Christ the Messiah or Gospel), and such acknowledgment (faith) produces good works without the intention toward the reward of salvation, because faith is a trust only known by an individual (in interpersonal basis) and his/her God or creator so that good works become not an exhibition of faith but an intuitive and unconditional expression of the personal bond and acknowledgment of the righteousness of God. So, the good works of an atheist who denied the existence of God couldn't possibly merit salvation; however, nobody could force what God would save for the reason that God reserves all the rights of whatever he deems to do; even the biblical theology admitted this notion—read Romans 9:15-18 of the Christian Bible.

In the present era, it's evident that the resurgence of the concept of legalism or Pharisee(ism) remains the archenemy of the message of justification by faith. The nature and force of legalism is centered on the coercive observance of the law with the intent for salvation, regardless of its inflictions on individual liberty or freedom. The prohibition of prostitution is just one classical litmus test of religious intolerance of the innocuous exercise of individual rights. Perhaps the modern-day legalists or scribes and Pharisees really know the nonexistence of the biblical Christ; perhaps, they know that the biblical Christ is nothing but a literary masterpiece with theological ramifications. And regardless of the vulnerable portrayal of the biblical Christ by Judeo-Christian theology, that it couldn't possibly stand the legitimate scientific scrutiny or any serious decent ordinary reason, the theory of Christism could provide the necessary defense to satisfy any doubt regarding the veritable or highest probability of the existence of God. So, even if the biblical Christ is true or not, the concept of justification by faith as a direct result or outcome of the Gospel of the Messiah is a message that has direct relevance with the most advance theory of the Cosmic Christ according to the concept of Christism with regard to the existence of God.

The Spirit of the Cosmic Christ couldn't be much more sensitive than loving, forgiving, compromising, and merciful with regard to the freedom of perception as to what human beings could attribute to the embodiment of the existence of God's. So, even if there existed various perceptions of the embodiment of God's existence or nature, the intent of worship outweighs the minor frailty of religious observance or liturgy. Even with the primitive form of religions, among its members or proponents, individual sincerity or intent (to whom) of worship remains the only basis of salvation, so in all religious organizations, a member could be only either: a faithful one—as a member or an individual whose intent of worship and observance of religious rites is for the acknowledgment of the existence of God or creator; or a religious materialist—as a member or an individual whose intent of worship and observance of religious rites is for salvation and material gain and/or of the amenities for the personal resolution of spiritual insecurity. However, God must always have the propriety to exercise judicial exception of the assessment for the appropriation of the reward for salvation. But at all times and applicable to all religious concepts, the message of justification by faith is the general arbiter or determinant of salvation, not only of the fact that the origin of sin, as primarily selfishness or exceeding greed—as stipulated in the structure of morality—is as ancient as the oldest civilization that has a formal religious belief or concept, but also of the corrupting influence inherent with the concept of salvation by works or the concept that God demands or requires works for salvation. Therefore, in a way or in different fashion, the concept of the sanctuary in the Old Testament of the Judeo-Christian Scripture could also have been practiced in principle by primitive religions such that all forms of religious concepts that give offerings to God to obtain salvation thereby categorically conform with the principle of religious materialism.

In this study, the sin of the concept of unilateral materialism, spiritualism, also the religious materialist has been portrayed in Judeo-Christian Scripture as the scribes and Pharisees. On the other hand, the message of the justification by faith is portrayed by the Gospel of the biblical Jesus Christ. These two diametrical concepts of salvation by works vs. justification (salvation) by faith or the Old and New Testament theologies of the Bible also in principle practically or theoretically reside in all religious beliefs or concepts. And as has been stipulated in this study, the existence of God is more likely than not, whether in terms of pure philosophy or physical perception.

Doubt of the existence of God probably doesn't have as much of a corrupting influence on human lives than on how various religions treat or treated the problem of human mortality. Salvation, no matter what its form, mechanics, or methodology, became the universal concept or language to which the solution of the problem of human mortality has been attributed. But even if the concept of the existence of God existed first, the corrupting influence of the concept of salvation by work doesn't necessarily affect its inherent unavoidable nature.

The biblical theology stipulated in the book of Genesis that the concept or perception of the existence of God existed first, and the concept or reality of salvation was brought about by the transgression of the law of God. Even perhaps with all the concepts of religions, the perception of the existence of God might have existed first, and the concept of salvation was triggered by the perception of guilt and human mortality. And in the course of time, the motive and amenities of the promise or proposition of salvation became the major concern that made a systematic climb into a height or proportion as a simple or sophisticated liturgy/creed regarded by most if not all religions as mandatory for salvation or theologically as the concept of righteousness by the law of work. The essential need or impulse for salvation or immortality is basically inherently of human nature (as stipulated in this study of the Structure of Morality).

The natural basic impulse or desire for immortality (salvation) must not be the predominant principle for the faith or love in/of God; otherwise, we violate or defile the justice and holy nature of the character of the creator and at the same time offend our own human nature. The inherent presence in human beings of the perception of the existence of God is the major element of what separates human beings from all the rest of the creatures in the solar system. The natural impulse or desire of immortality or salvation is basically the outworking of the co-driver impulse of self-preservation. The Russian psychologist/physiologist, Ivan Pavlov, who attended church and theological seminary, perhaps clearly understood the relationship of the instinct of self-preservation and the concept of the mentality of righteousness by the law or work, as manifested in his study of the conditioned reflex, popularly known experiment as the Pavlov dog. Regardless of the practical use of the theory of conditioned reflex, it has a tremendous detrimental effect or poses a great infliction against the holy nature of God's character: that God never coerces or makes any insinuation thereof is evident in the natural desire of freedom that's inherent in human nature. Even in the Judeo-Christian biblical theology in the creation of Adam and Eve in the Garden of Eden, the concept of freedom has been bestowed to the first couple; otherwise, they couldn't have had the capacity to have transgressed.

Regardless that the concept of the existence of God and freedom are inseparable, it's rather pathetic that both religion and democratic forms of governments, despite the message of the Gospel or justification by faith, a whole lot of innocuous freedom is being deprived of individuals. The most sensitive and classical incident of this is the intolerance against sexual prostitution (Matthew 21:31), because to God, religious materialism is more unpardonable, because the human being is not God's Pavlov dog. Salvation is not a merchandise to be bought or sold by the desire of materialism or immortal self-preservation. It's a gift for those who believe in the person and righteousness of God. God didn't intend our inherent human instincts to be coercive mechanism to seek God for the reason that a human has the ability and capacity of self-realization to judge and control one's beliefs for evil or for good—or to believe or deny God.

The concept of the buying or merchandising of morality is a variation of the application of the concept of conditioned reflex by Ivan Pavlov. At the expense of freedom, the application of the concept of conditioned reflex to human beings could produce a culture or society practicing robotic moralism. Although this practical benefit is mostly directly beneficial to authority and leaders of society and even to society in general in terms of material and moral management, on the contrary, the subtle destruction of freedom is a direct persecution of the message of the justification by faith. The merchandising of morality, even if it's transacted under the name of Christ and/or religion, is the arch anti-Christ itself. Because the theory of the message of the Gospel or justification by faith is the last, ultimate, or supreme argument of truth of the perception of the righteousness and the nature of the existence of God, hence, all religious practices must be judged by it, as the final arbiter of truth for the evaluation of the ways and means of salvation. The buying of morality is not any different as an anti-Gospel from the concept of the selling of indulgences in the fifteenth century. Likewise, the concept of freedom is the highest argument for the most rational status of existence of the individual or between individuals or group of individuals. Without the concept of liberty, individuals become completely mechanically subservient to the law of authoritarianism, and it is such a condition the practice of religion could either completely deny or impose by government authority or its designated clergy. The Old Testament biblical theology' itself came from such a condition or concept; however, the New Testament redeemed some of the theological faults of its past so that the Gospel is a comprehensive salvation except to the scribes

133

and Pharisees or the legalists whose professions posed conflicts with the message of justification by faith or the Gospel.

In an insightful analysis, any government or social imposition of religion to an individual is a complete anathema to the concept of the existence of God or specifically with the message of justification by faith. The concept of freedom and the existence of God must always be concurrent, and this argument is the direct opponent of the concept of unilateral scientific, social-political (communism/socialism), or religious (Jewish Pharisee[ism]) materialism. As has been stipulated in this study with the discussion of the structure of morality, communism or socialism is derivative of the instinct of altruism and acquiescence is subordinate with the instinct of conscience and the power of choice (freedom) as the main driving impulse of democratic government or/with the real concept of the existence of God.

All philosophy has a core of origin and impetus which is primarily based on the search of the nature of existence, and all assumptions or hypotheses must be comprehensive or unified in scope such that any local concept of existence must find complete relevancy with the nature of universal existence. An instance of this notion is the human instinct of self-preservation or to the extent of the desire of immortal existence by which all religious campaigns under the name of salvation.

Because the biblical (Judeo-Christian) theology the most sophisticated form of presentation of the concept or relationship of salvation and the existence of God, it's one or the intents of this study to find the main thesis or major argument if Christianity could embrace the theory of Christism (this study itself) in terms of both philosophical contention and practical utility. And only the concept of the Gospel or justification by faith or biblical theology is reconciled to this study (Christism) and such a concept (justification by faith) could only find relevance under the administration of freedom under a government ruled with a concept of democracy. Perhaps it's the concept of justification by faith that produced the separation of church and state and democratic forms of government. But regardless of how the democratic form of government came about or originated/proliferated, in any serious and honest scrutiny or inquiry of reason that has the full determination of the search of the truth (existence), the concept of the existence of God and freedom will eventually emanate. Fortunately, the concept of the existence of God and freedom came about before serious scientific knowledge proliferated.

Any individual who hadn't given serious thought or consideration to the ultimate argument of the message of the Gospel or justification by faith will remain with an opinion of religious materialism (in pure religion) or the government imposition of religion (in the pursuit of social moral management and power) or socialism and communism to the extent of a concept of the nonexistence of God and believe that there's a morality or virtue of the spirit without the presence of freedom; even animals resent unduly physical restrictions. Materialism is the only cause and basis of all moral corruptions of human existence. In religion it's based solely on the merchandising of the concept of salvation. The desire of salvation has become the principal search and motive for the love of God. Human love toward his creator has become conditional on the reward of salvation, which is not only conflicting to the nature of the message of the Gospel or justification by faith of the unconditional love of God toward man but also of human rationality or propriety of the honest search of the highest or ultimate truth. If God demands the works of faith, then it's no longer faith, but rather that faith obey and/or seek the righteousness of God. The righteousness of God is love. God is love. If God saved man without preconditions or conditions, then man should also love God unconditional of salvation. Good works, therefore, are the result of faith of the realization of the concept of being saved of the unconditional love of God: Apostle Paul, in his epistle to the Romans, argued that while we were yet sinners, Christ died for us. If righteousness or good works is the fruit of faith and love of God, the concept of the complete separation of church and state must always be inevitable and indispensable to separate the interest of spiritual righteousness from worldly motives so individuals may devote themselves to following the message of the Gospel without conflict of interest because the merchandising of morality or righteousness by work is a complete anathema or diametrical to the intent of righteousness by faith. Those who believe and advocate that righteousness by faith and righteousness of the obedience of the law (works) could be reconciled at a middle ground is committing hypocrisy of the highest degree. It must be understood that the only viable reason for the existence of a structured government is of the only fact that human existence remained sinful and mortal, but in the coming immortal dimension of reality, the need of government would be completely vain for the very reason that only those who honestly love God would be saved, for there would be no room for a materialist in the new order of reality called eternal existence.

There would be no other ultimate message other than the pure unadulterated argument of justification by faith that could be derived by the use of the purpose of reason inherently provided to human beings by God himself. And this study of Christism provided the ultimate probability of the existence of God so that even if the Jesus event of the Bible didn't really take place, humanity has a hope of immortality. And those who died before hearing the faith according to this study but believed full-heartedly (honestly) of the Gospel of the biblical Jesus Christ, or just simply wholeheartedly believed in the existence of God for other religious concepts, would receive the blessing of salvation or immortality. It's only through the concept or message of justification by faith that all religious concepts or the biblical Gospel of the Christians that God could possibly determine the sincerity of an individual's faith or believe in God; otherwise, He (creator) had intentionally inscribed the instinct of the absolute (impertinent of choice or freedom) desire of salvation (ultimate self-preservation) so that a human being is no different than any other creation, and Ivan Pavlov's theory of "conditioned reflex" governs all religious motives and pursuits.

Before we draw the line between the sharp contrast of the message of justification by faith and all forms of materialism, including the concept of righteousness by work, it must be noted that it's not only the Old Testament theology of the Judeo-Christian Scripture that holds the concept of salvation by way of offering and sacrifices to gain the favor of God. The New Testament of the Bible of the Judeo-Christians found the fundamental error of the Old Testament, which is the concept of righteousness by work, and offered a new concept of justification by faith through the crucifixion (offering/sacrifice) act of the savior Jesus Christ—the lamb of God—that has done away with or abolished the concept of sanctuary or offering to gain the favor of God's mercy and salvation.

The concept of the existence of God and its antithesis, the nonexistence of God, are the only two major concepts as the basis and impetus upon all reason, philosophy, perception, or argument of the nature of existence. Therefore, if God exists, he couldn't just afford to be just an innocent bystander watching the powerless individuals being taken advantage of in the name of God by the ruler or leaders of society. God, in a way, must have inspired those who have formulated the concept of justification by faith so that freedom, reason, justice, fairness, love, forgiveness, humility, etc. must be understood as the nature of the righteousness of God. The concept of justification by faith, if understood properly, couldn't be used by materialistic leaders whose intention of leadership is for self-glorification, power, and financial gains.

Without the message of justification by faith, there's no other method or opinion to fight the corrupting influences of unilateral materialism, and those who propose the theory must have possessed complete honesty and faith in the existence of God. But has the Gospel or the message of justification by faith been contrived or produced as a philosophy or theology for a self-defense mechanism for the anticipated advancement of knowledge? Is the message of justification by faith a subtle contrivance of the sole purpose of the perpetuation of organized religion? This serious inquiry couldn't be verified, but regardless, or whether or not the biblical Jesus Christ event took place, there's no reason to discount the existence of God. One of the intents of this study is for the vindication of the truth, especially with the concept of righteousness by faith which is the sole theology that could set us free from the coercion of liturgy and spiritual bondage under the administration of a hierarchy of power, However, all religious rites and liturgies could remain observed and dedicated to God as long as they are stricken out under the name and merchandising of salvation because the justice and love of God will save those who have offerings/sacrifices as well as those who have not.

If the biblical Gospel of Jesus Christ has been contrived by organized religion in their time, they have made the most grievous error, because if the Gospel was a fabrication for the preservation of organized religion, it is itself a self-destruction of any organized religion if the message of the Gospel or justification by faith would be understood by individuals of its profound meaning or implications. Sometimes the truth reveals itself amazingly, even in the most unexpected situations or circumstances, so that only those who are genuinely truthful, honest, and who search for reason become wise and thereby could make a real distinction of the real implications of the ultimate truth of the existence and righteousness of God. In this regard, the message of justification by faith, although born with the Jews or Hebrews, and the concept of the existence of God are its proprietary driving mechanism, but it's the concept of salvation that corrupted most if not all religious concepts.

There is no excuse for any individual not be able to understand the simple message of justification by faith; it's only the corrupting influence and charm of all forms of materialism which could prevent individuals from the truth. It's only the message of justification by faith that could usher in the distinction between those who really unconditionally love the Lord against the religious materialist. When an individual completely understands the Gospel (righteousness by faith) he can no longer be corrupted by the materialism, thereby having gained ultimate truth would prevails be blessed for eternal salvation in the immortal dimension of reality. When an individual or group of individuals completely understand justification by faith and live a life of the Gospel, he or she is either loved or persecuted. Perhaps the New Testaments writers of the Judeo-Christian Scriptures were really ardently promoting the message of the Gospel or justification faith; perhaps they were faithful and honest with the ultimate search of the truth that they encountered persecution and antagonism among the Old Testament's Jewish traditionalists and derision (Corinthians 1:23; Romans I : 16-17) from the Greek intellectualism because of the direct anti-materialistic nature of the Gospel message, so that if any honest and devout follower of the message must by all means carry the cross (its significance) of Christ. The Gospel isn't in any circumstance an insinuation of liberation from doing good works, but that good works or righteousness by the obedience of the law are relegated out as the primary means of salvation and as the intent of worship to the concept of faith or of the existence of God. However, the Gospel or justification by faith also aren't an imposition to abandon the reasonable or necessary requirements of material existence, regardless of the heavy exhortation of New Testament theology against worldliness (Romans 12:2).

The concept of justification by faith is not a proprietary property of Judeo-Christian religion. In fact, all religious concepts of the existence of God must originated with a rudimentary concept of faith until such an unforeseen event took place that the concept of salvation took the prominent concern or status that prevailed with the practice of religion. On this basis or argument of a unified corruption or deterioration of the intent of worship of most if not all religious concepts, likewise, the sole redemption of humanity is based on the argument of justification by faith or the Gospel. It, therefore, became evident that there was only one source/cause of transgression: materialism and its various forms. In fact, the Judeo-Christians couldn't be more succinct and precise than in saying that the original sin was selfishness (greed and envy, the sin of Lucifer) as argued in the Bible. This transgression took various subtle forms across human activities, lifestyles, philosophies, ambitions, etc., and it has been presented here in this study with concept of the structure of morality and also with the sin of materialism and spiritualism. Because there's only one cause of human transgressions, there's only one concept of redemption. Redemption is for humanity to go back with its original unconditional love to his creator by which the main objective of the unconditional love of God toward us couldn't be more ultimately expressed by the sacrifice of our savior Jesus Christ with the Judeo-Christian or biblical theology as the concept of justification or righteousness by faith. Because there's only one major cause of sin, because there's only one God, there's only one absolute concept of redemption.

Epilogue

In religion there's no higher theology or concept of the existence of God than justification by faith (John 19:30). It's a form of sacrifice because the truth and righteousness and justice of God is honesty and fairness, or simply unconditional love, and every individual or religious concept must be judged according to this principle. The purity of the message of justification by faith is that it's not an ideal, creed, or dogma but a personal, unconditional relationship to a creator called God. Faith, therefore, doesn't demand a reward of salvation for good works performed but rather that worship is an unconditional duty to a creator whose righteousness is unconditional love. Is it conceivable that a creator would reward eternal death to his creature who served him unconditionally? Only those who have no faith and trust would believe so. It's redundantly reiterated in this study that even if the biblical Jesus Christ event didn't really take place, the message of justification by faith is sufficient to give us hope of immortality because the Cosmic Christ does exist as it has been stipulated in the beginning of the study of Christism.

The message of justification by faith is mandatory for salvation primarily because of the fact that if immortality would be realized, there wouldn't be any form of government. Self-governing would because love would be the only ruler in paradise; there would be no form of worship to God, but every individual would be dedicated to the caring of creation (for God himself is the whole creation). And only the message of justification by faith could prepare humanity for such an immoral state of reality. Even if the concept of justification by faith was a contrivance by organized, powerful religious individuals in their time, the message of justification by faith transpire beyond deception because the ultimate truth could never be corrupted. The existence of the search of the ultimate truth is the very evidence that God exist with an embodiment of the whole universal phenomena. The mystery that we are thinking, and rational living creatures is the evidence that the universe itself possesses the same condition on the basis that a unified nature of a universal existence—that the nature of atomic structures and energy forms in universally identical. Because of the huge embodiment of God that couldn't possibly transform into a form that fits the limited human sight it is much more impossible to believe that humanity could travel far beyond the universe(s) and take a photograph of the cosmos or universes; it requires a great deal of faith to believe in the existence of God.

The struggle of faith will remain the same: it will continue between those who unconditionally love God with the truth of justification by faith against the proponents of righteousness by work or religious materialists—the modem-day Sadducees and Pharisees. In the modern time, it's evident that the real pure message of justification by faith remains rejected; regardless that it's being preached, it's very much adulterated with the concept of salvation by works. This is the most subtle form of adultery or moral or spiritual prostitution (the harlot in the book of Revelation). The biblical theology itself talked about virgins: 14:4; Matthew 25—the parable of the ten virgins. Even Jesus Christ was born from a virgin (Matthew 1:23). The implication virginity is certainly very clear as the most explicit exposition of the truth of the direct antipathy of the doctrine of justification (righteousness) by faith versus righteousness by work. And there's no religious concept that could deny or sidestep this ultimate quest of truth or the full verity of reason. Even on the physiological argument of this study that during the coming immortal dimension of reality we shall all become virgins to start a new immortal generation, the truth of justification by faith serves a dual motive to prepare those who would be saved in the coming immortal state of reality.

The process of God's election for immortality commenced since the foundation of civilization, and the only medium of judgment remains the same: the message of justification by faith. The biblical theology also confirms this concept that the plan of salvation began since the foundation of the world began and is also confirmed by the theory that Christ is the alpha and the omega, which is a direct revelation that the *plan* of creation is complete (would be completed) which contains both the mortal and immortal state, which is an exposition of the coherent nature of the truth. As stipulated in this study, truth could only be perceived if its existing or assumed antithesis is preconceived or understood into consideration, as also with the evidence of the inherent preexistence of conscience the knowledge of good and evil or right or wrong.

Human perception is basically and inherently inculcated into innate nature by the creator and itself became the battleground of corruption and righteousness, therefore, also for the election of salvation for immortality. The only demand of salvation or immortality is purity of spirit: an individual capable of self-governing by the statute of unconditional love from the pure and unadulterated message of justification by faith. Because in the coming immortal life there will be no need of government, nor will man be subjected to power or law. Under this condition only the message of justification by faith could provide humanity the necessary preparation and understanding. Its antithesis, righteousness by work, could only lead to the development of robotic moralism: a situation of "conditioned reflex" as in the experiments by Pavlov and Pavlov's dog.

Righteousness by work will only be a viable alternative situation if the immortal reality would be governed by technology.

The ultimate purpose of the message of justification by faith, as it has been stipulated here, in this study, constitutes complex issues, although it seems simple, it is actually the only other half of the highest consideration of philosophy or reason of the nature of universal and local existence as a unified or single phenomena. As has been stated earlier, the truth of justification by faith as stipulated by the Judeo-Christian theology with the embodiment of the biblical Jesus Christ, is the ultimate and last argument of salvation with the promise of the restoration of the Garden of Eden, a situation of human immortal existence without government, regardless that the former has one law, the latter must have none.

Because all of the knowledge of good and evil is the result of reason and the direct interpretation or understanding of the present nature of existence, and that the present must judge historical events, therefore, reason finds an absolute relationship between the past, present, and future with certainty or with faith or with reason and a maximum allowable amount of skepticism or doubt. Although it is possible to have an absolute faith, and even biblical theology asserts the power of such a faith (Matthew 17:20), such faith couldn't be found today, if there was one in the past. If ever absolute faith may be attainable, its reward is hope in the future, because if the reward (power) is now, then it presents a danger with the nature of faith itself in this present mortal dimension of reality for the reason that it creates the dilemma that the human is nothing but God's Pavlovian dog. And in such a situation faith would cease to exist of its necessity and purpose of pure and honest election for salvation, and such an episode (mystical reality) only exists in the immortal state of reality.

The sole continuing objective (and source) of faith, therefore, is not the concept of salvation but the acknowledgment of the existence of God because the only option of a way to know God is to understand God himself, which is through universal creation which itself is the embodiment of the Son of God (the Cosmic Christ). Such a query is

143

an innate element of human nature so that even with those who tried to evade answering the question, their act of evasion is itself an evident part of the inherent nature of inquiry because the argument of choosing not to know is an inherent antithesis component of choosing to know. Therefore, the existence of reason is evidence of the existence of God or a creator, and the justice of God is evidence of the presence of the concept of freedom because freedom itself is life for God is life or creation. And those who don't believe in the existence of God and freedom and confirm that they have the right to belief of their opinions already contradicted themselves.

Why is faith necessary? All forms of perceptions or understanding inherently contain diametrical components or a thesis and its antithesis. Therefore, faith is the only mechanism by which a decision is made necessary for election for salvation. Because faith in God is made known through the derivative of reason, it must have a purpose but for the election for immortality. Mortality, therefore, is to know God, while immortality (future event) is the reward that we have known and acknowledged God. Such consideration inspires an honest believer to uphold the truth and render unconditional (not withstanding of salvation) worship or love to his creator and to creation in general. Any individual who doesn't believe the concept of unconditional love is a religious materialist. And this is the message of the unconditional love and amazing grace of God manifested by the Gospel or the sacrifice of the cross of the biblical Christ. But even if the biblical or Judeo-Christian Jesus Christ event didn't actually take place, it's the same message that the Cosmic Christ demands for salvation. The message of justification by faith extends its profound significance as the only mechanism for humanity to respect and preserve universal creation with absolute equality and freedom of existence among universal residents. Otherwise, technology and hierarchy are the only other antithetical probabilities of the future for whether immortality would be available through the ultimate advancement of technology or that the Garden of Eden concept would actually happen or be restored or be stated if it does not have an actual historical event. If immortality and the Garden of Eden concept would be realized, it would be a sole act of God. Eternal life or immortality of physical existence is an argument beyond the complete elimination of pathogens and the aging process; it requires the mystery of recreation by a creator because of the fact that the existence of the solar system is contingent upon universal phenomena. This is the message of justification by faith which is extendible beyond the understanding and concept of biblical theology.

Justification by faith according to this study of Christism is a message of trust and belief that the Cosmic Christ who sometime in the future will render immortality to individuals discriminately relevant to one's intent of faith. Otherwise, God couldn't have provided man the capacity of reason, and on the basis that God's only medium of instruction is through perception or understanding, which is itself the nature of existence as trinitarian: that all creation with or without the capacity of reason is the product of the purpose of God the father (the nothing or void) and the son of God (the matter). Reason, therefore, is itself the Holy Spirit provided only in human beings; for reason always pursues the truth. Because reason with freedom has the capacity for misunderstanding or the commission of evil is available, without it the Holy Spirit couldn't be holy or just. So, the Holy Spirit (reason/perception) could either be used for good or bad, Human beings were given the capacity of reason— meaning the gift of the Holy Spirit; any other creatures below the rank of human being are incapable of understanding or the perception of the nature of creation, thereby lacking the capacity of faith or belief in God. And such a belief in God during the coming reign of immortality, for which a situation of existence by which faith (became necessary) will be glorified, reason/perception will in turn become homogeneous— meaning righteousness or good could only exist, and all past memory of existence during the mortal state of reality would serve as "read-only memory" and could no longer be made available to affect perception in the immortal state of being. The concept that memory during the mortal dimension of reality has a necessity of existence as "read-only memory" in the immortal dimension warrants the argument that every individual elected for immortality must retain their original personality, otherwise, what purpose would it serve to be saved? And why did God not instead create a robot in the first place if all he required was a creature to fulfill eternal worship only for his glory?

The primary role of the Holy Spirit is for the understanding and acknowledgment of the existence and purpose of God but not to serve his own purpose. It therefore became evident that the Holy Spirit inspired, endorsed, and supported the message of justification by faith, regardless of the intent of its framers how it was originally cultivated. The message transcends any intentional or otherwise culpable human materialistic ambition, in contrast to the concept of righteousness by work, which is nothing but an extension of the intrinsic desire of self-preservation—which is also salvation or immortality. Regardless that self-preservation is also provided by God in human nature, it has no salvation value, because even the animals and all the creatures below humans have the same instinct or desires. The great Apostle Paul of the Judeo-Christian Scriptures tried to define or understand the corruption of human nature in 1 Corinthians 2:10, 14.

The Old Testament of the Judeo-Christian Scriptures perfectly illustrated the selfishness of human nature when human beings worshiped God in terms of the concept of salvation through the obedience of the law and the offering of sacrifices. Despite all the attempts to please God for salvation, their concerted efforts to procure immortality weren't realized because sin and mortality remained; fortunately, the concepts of hope remained. But in the New Testament they crucified their God. Mystery of mystery; "Father forgive them; for they know not what they do." Again, despite all of the miracles of the New Testament and the presence of God in their midst whom they crucified; the Jewish/Israel nation didn't obtain immortality. Hope remained embedded with the concept of the second coming of Christ. It might be hard or easy to find the rationality of the relationship of the first and second comings of Christ, and perhaps all the majesty of miracles of biblical theology, but of the concept of justification by faith which is a verity applicable to all religious concepts of the ultimate query of the existence of God, if complete honesty is allowed to dominate one's perception of the final truth so that whether the biblical Jesus Christ event took place or not the overriding principle of justification by faith is the only viable underwriter or determinant of ultimate philosophical argument between forgery and truth of the concept of the existence of God; for the message of justification by faith clearly illustrates the difference between those who have understood the nature of existence (God and creation) and those who deliberately neglected to know according to the prompting of reason or Holy Spirit of God.

Even if the biblical Jesus Christ has a historical actual existence, the argument for evidences and/or the nature of the present era of the complete withdrawal (or nonexistence) of mysteries and manifestations of the claim of past events couldn't be rationally condemned against an individual's prospect of salvation. This study (Christism) is never intended as a dogmatic or idealistic presentation of the quest for truth, but primarily to probe the best probability of the existence of a creator through the nature of creation—and with the purpose of reason (not as an incidental occurrence) only available in human beings. And only human beings are capable of the perception of faith in God, not irrelevant coincidence that human beings are the end of God's act of creation. The concept of the perception of faith, therefore, is the primary objective of all creation thereby origin of all matter and existence. Righteousness by work (as the antithesis of the concept of justification by faith) is the most subtle form (the spiritual harlot in the book of Revelation, Chapter 17) of the concept of materialism.

Even if the biblical Jesus Christ did actually exist, the argument of why (how) the technical explanation of creation wasn't made available to humanity, but rather the whole Old and New Testament theologies dealt mainly with the moral aspect of existence and is completely silent on all the technical aspects of immortality. On the other hand, scientific wisdom and rationality completely disagreed with biblical theology of creation and mysticism. However, scientific wisdom or reason couldn't have followed the guidance of the Holy Spirit of God; therefore, it's a complete misunderstanding of the truth as it's evident that scientific speculations presently rely on the theory of materialism of the nature of existence and thereby avoided the concept of the existence of God. Therefore, this study of Christism, which clearly explained the faults of both unilateral materialism and spiritualism when embraced by any individual honestly seeking the truth, couldn't possibly be guilty of jeopardizing or risking one's prospect of salvation regardless or even if there was an actual historical Gospel event that took place, but if there wasn't and the Cosmic Christ is alive, as has been stipulated in this study, then there also will be a final decisive judgment against the sin of materialism both religious, scientific, or otherwise.

All philosophy which honestly seeks the absolute truth of the nature of existence couldn't possibly avoid not dealing with the dilemma of the existence of the void, nothing, or immaterial force because it's the only proposition that could resolve the dilemma of the existence of infinity for, they are one and the same. There's not a viable concept of the existence of matter or something, without the presence of infinity or void for the very concept that matter couldn't possibly have an infinite mass. And the very fact that humanity is awarded with the perception of matter, which doesn't indispensably require the concept of faith, human reason, or rationality to exactly know without a doubt of his physical reality; on the contrary, humanity has no physical perception of the void or infinity and/or by which, on the same token, that the concept of faith has relevance. It's also in the same regard that human existence has a perception of mortality or death which deals with the issue that the existence of matter is completely dependent upon the existence of the void, for without such rationality there would be no other proposition that humanity could be prompted to try to understand and believe of the necessity to know God the Father or the void, and humanity wouldn't have a perception of immortality. It's therefore evident that there exists a unified purpose of the present state and nature of existence. In fact, scientific wisdom also lends itself to a mortal universe as evident in the theory of the black hole, regardless that its theorist misunderstood the very nature of existence by failing to solve the dilemma of infinity.

In the immortal reality or dimension in which the gods dwell, there's no annihilating opposing forces in terms of permanent destruction. It's only in the present mortal dimension that the perception of opposing forces of eternal destruction are perceived by sciences; therefore the concepts of evil is only a concept of behavior or action fully derivative of the erroneous understanding and application of the innate structure of morality (see Structure of Morality)—likewise with the concept of righteousness or good, that is the appropriate and balanced approach of a lifestyle is a direct result of one's virtues and responsibility with the innate structure of morality. Regardless that all the functions, operations, or activities of all creation are sanctioned by the deity, and that all creation is the creation of God, the choices and liberty of the direction and pathways of behavior, including the making of intelligent decisions, is as the sole discretion of the individual; therefore, it would be misunderstanding of reality to give or issue physical attributes of evil or it would be condemning to insinuate a proposition that the nothing or infinity is evil as an antithesis of matter. The fact that matter couldn't possibly exist without the void or nothing or infinity issues validity that there's no antithesis of God. In like manner, when salvation for immortality will arrive, its antithesis could no longer exist in terms of eternity.

Faith of its ultimate origin and consideration must be the main intent of creation. Faith is the only viable explanation of the nature of existence, as well as the highest rational condition of whom salvation would be granted or awarded. Faith is not a conditioned reflex but rather a condition of freedom without condition, for it's completely a voluntary response without the stimulus of reward. but its object is appreciation and acknowledgment of a creature to a creator or God. Because human beings are awarded with the tremendous capacity to procure an adequate philosophical understanding of the nature of the universal phenomena by virtue of his own choice or liberty, it is itself the evidence that the reward of salvation would be a random selection and not generally imposed as obligatory, coerced. or managed; otherwise, there's no relevance of the concept of individual choice/freedom and personal responsibility and accountability or even faith. If God originally created human creation as a moral robot, then nobody could have perceived the concept of freedom, and God didn't intend for humans to be robots as it's evident that coercion communism, and socialism existed. Furthermore, nobody could possibly coerce (nor have the knowledge) without freedom. so that if the original intent of creation is robotic moralism, then freedom couldn't be understood, but the original intent of creation is for faith and faith couldn't honestly exist without freedom, coercion, robotic moralism, righteousness by work was given their choices to act as their own discretion. This is the justice and righteousness of God which is evident in the existence of those who have the concept of unconditional faith. The definition of unconditional faith or love—devotion—is a concept that answers the question of why a creature should necessarily demand from his creator Doesn't the creator know everything? And on the other hand, why should God necessarily demand from a creature who has a pure intent of faith? Didn't the creator give humanity reason and the intellectual capacity to understand what is evil and good? In fact, faith couldn't find rationality and relevance with the presence of demand, and response to a demand has no value regardless of intent and honesty because demand preempts the value of intent. The concept of the separation of work and faith has been stipulated by Apostle Paul. These criteria of salvation aren't as easy as it seems to comprehend, but it's the only way by which reason or the Holy Spirit could determine who is to be saved, as has been stipulated by the concept of the wise and foolish virgins waiting for the coming of salvation (Revelation 14:4; Matthew 25).

It's so obvious why righteousness by works isn't the determinant for salvation. Righteousness by works is not only a demand of/from hierarchy but also a systematic, dogmatic, and managed (on some occasion coerced) system of the concept of salvation, regardless that it embraces the concept of God. The Holy Spirit of God isn't an unsympathetic and indifferent bystander; in fact, historical evidence points to and indicates the dramatic shift of theology of the Old and New Testaments of the Bible considered as one of the most sophisticated religious systems ever founded: the Judeo- Christian faith. Because of the inherent tendency of human nature to violate or corrupt moral objective with regard to his own human nature, the Spirit of God occasionally intercedes through human nature so that the truth must be available to be chosen for those who will choose with respect to freedom and liberty. The truth is not a foreign or mysterious event but rather an inherent part of human nature (see Structure of Morality).

The truth is faith, faith of the existence of God. True faith is a dynamic force in human nature because it produces hope and love, which leads to respect to the preservation of creation. Because all human behavior is a direct result of a conscious and/or subconscious driving impulse of priority and inspiration, faith is one of the conscious human impulses which established man to acknowledge his creator. When a true faith is established, a personal relationship with God is perceived. This is the vertical relationship between man and God or the relationship of the acknowledgment that man is a creature, and that God is his creator Because the life of all creatures is dependent upon their creator through the prompting of reason or the Holy Spirit of God, even the single-cell organism is controlled by purpose. The fact is that all creation is a purpose, and such a purpose is the will and force of God. The presence of faith in human nature could either be accepted, preserved, or denied through the gift or impulse of freedom of the free will. Therefore, the denial of reason or the Holy Spirit of God could lead to the violation of the proper observance of the structure of morality, and if an individual even goes to the extent to deny the driving impulse of self-preservation, it leads to self-destruction. All of human nature is given by God because there's nothing that man created for himself (in terms of origin of energy) nor that man created himself.

Because the structure of morality defines the development of human beings, all human beings at some point in their lives couldn't avoid dealing with the prompting of reason or he Holy Spirit, whether to accept faith or deny it. Therefore, there's only one origin of the concept of the existence of God because all religious concepts started from within the human being, and not as a written code dropped from a mysterious realm above, but rather it's already inscribed in the human gene and inspired by way of reason or the Holy Spirit of God. Because the Holy Spirit of God is also the reason which enables the perception of conscience or right and wrong and all the rest of human perception of the self and consciousness and its environment, the Holy Spirit or reason, therefore, is also a universal phenomenon, and in particular in human beings it inspires fully and not partially the inherent structure of morality but the actual reality of action or behavior is the direct result as the reaction, and its (absolutely individual/personal) distribution, interpretation, and management could either be good or bad—this is the human individual responsibility and accountability given under the provision of individual liberty/freedom. Although human beings have the perception of inspiration, they have no perception of another entity or alien spirit within him because the Holy Spirit doesn't speak about or for himself but rather leads one with the perception of the existence of God or faith. The presence of reason is the evidence of the existence of the Holy Spirit of God; otherwise, conscience, freedom, and faith couldn't be made available, and the absence of these is destruction and life couldn't have been possible because self-preservation and cell division, altruism and acquiescence are themselves integral parts of the manifestation of reason or purpose. And even an atheist or agnostic couldn't possibly believe that the process of cell division doesn't have any particular purpose. If chance, as evolutionist proposed, is the basis of existence, then existence could have been more chaotic. In order to be chance, its probability must defy existing preconditions and must not respect past, present, or future logics; therefore, chance couldn't or could hardly stay or remain coherent. The truth is, even the most rudimentary single-cell organism's life and behavior is fixed at certain parameters or conditions, regardless that in all life forms few anomalies are possible, but such a condition isn't a complete deviant from its predecessors. In order for chance to have credibility, a certain life form must be able to deviate completely from what is the present state or form of a cell structure. It must be considered that the cell structures of plant and animal cells are almost identical. This suggests that life could only exist in such a condition, at least from a human perspective or understanding. Basically, therefore, the probability of how life could be possible is dictated by one concept/purpose or a creator.

The relationship of general and specific inspirations of the Holy Spirit of God in human beings are both absolute and relative: absolute on the basis that the Holy Spirit generally inspires all creation for survival through the structure of morality, and specific on the basis that the Holy Spirit corresponds to individual desires, either good or evil. Good and evil, therefore, are completely of individual choice and the Holy Spirit of God could record all human understanding and actions. The Holy Spirit of God could be accessed through individual responses to the inspiration of faith, faith that's not defined by religious creeds or theological systems but by a personal (individual) relationship of man to his creator. Although, the Holy Spirit could be experienced through faith in individual, actual, physical life experiences, the process of how couldn't be. Human history has made a tremendous effort of trying to establish communication with the spirits of the gods and deceased human beings, but all have failed, in terms of mysterious manifestations, because human understanding of the nature of creation/universal existence was faulty. But for anybody to discount that the Holy Spirit of God could be experienced in the natural order of occurrence of actual physical human experiences, it's only because of the lack of real or true faith. Because faith has been understood as a dogma/doctrine of religious forms rather than a personal relationship with the creator, humanity will continue to be corrupted by the erroneous doctrines of spiritualism and materialism. Because faith becomes a dogma as a matter of absolute condition of salvation, humanity will continue to be worshipping religious forms rather that God. The understanding that God requires or demands a special place and form of worship, coupled with the idea that God's spirit could only be communicated through special procedures of meditation and religious liturgy, violates the concept of the message of justification by faith. One attempt to understand this situation is by the biblical presentation of the life and times of Jesus Christ in his encounters with his religious enemies like the scribes and Pharisees.

The idea that God demands or requires is the most basic misunderstanding of the nature of the righteousness of God, and it's the major cause of philosophical failure to understand the nature of faith. Worship and faith then assumed religious forms by which some are strict but most, if not all, become an absolute condition of salvation. Because salvation became a commodity to be achieved according to religious forms of liturgy or rites, and its dispensation could only come through religious authority and management, the exercise of faith, therefore, became available only through the transaction of a middleman. This idea is also repudiated by the concept of biblical theology of justification by faith by which Jesus Christ was ever the only mediator. In fact, that Jesus is the Messiah and high priest for man salvation is a concept supposedly meant to abolish all religious forms from the management of salvation. Anybody who would like to deny that the New Testament theology of the Bible inherently trying to convey that the concept of salvation had corrupted the concept of faith is doing so only because he probably knew that the Jesus event didn't take place and is in defiance of the message of justification by faith. The object of faith, therefore, became salvation and not the acknowledgment of the existence of God. This is religious materialism in the first degree, and relatively, it is no different from any other forms of materialism. In fact, the New Testament theology of the Christian Bible couldn't avoid Christ as the embodiment of its final doctrine; it's the very evidence that the truth is not, wasn't, or never will be in a form of dogma or creed. Yet despite this confirmation, affirmation, and foundation of truth, humanity's religious power of hierarchy continues to associate religious creed, doctrine, and liturgy as an integral part of the truth. This is a situation of spiritual adultery, and it's not any more worthy that those who fully believe that the truth assumed full religious form and ideology which is a situation of being the antichrist.

Knowledge and wisdom don't' create the truth but the truth that is inherently in all creation leads to knowledge and wisdom regardless that it could be rejected to be utilized or pursued (freedom). Because the spirit of God which is in all creation and which inspires the structure of morality in human beings is the only cause and giver of all knowledge and wisdom, the impulse to seek the truth is part of the truth because the truth is already made and not to be made. Humanity was given the liberty of perception to be able to see and understand (or refuse to understand) the truth but not to produce the truth because creation is a finished concept of God. Truth, therefore, is the acknowledgment of the existence of God. Perception is knowledge and wisdom as the eye of faith similar to the physical eye which connects to the physical reality. As the physical eye doesn't create what it sees, so knowledge doesn't create the truth. Because human physical (matter) and spiritual (spirit) perception resides in one unified dimension of reality, one could not be without the other. This is the unified theory of existence as stipulated in this study. The same principle applies to universal phenomena overall: that the existence of matter and the void or nothing could only exist one with the other. This exposition revealed the fallacy of the concept of unilateral materialism as well as the theory of spiritualism. There's no substantial confirmation of the existence of the infinity of matter nor has there been confirmed evidence of the possibility of the existence of spirit outside matter (even the spirit of God the father—the nothing or void—must interact with the son of God the universal physical matter for its existence. Humanity has failed to understand his nature by trying to avoid it. The existence of mortality befuddled and vexed human consciousness so that when humanity admitted no hope (the nonexistence of God), it resulted in and admitted the logic of materialism. On the other hand, spiritualism's refusal to accept mortality thereby cursed the flesh or matter proclaiming liberation at post-mortem. But the worst-case scenarios are the concepts of religious materialists, the spiritual adulterers or harlots and hypocrites to whom even the biblical New Testament theology proclaimed that they couldn't enter the kingdom of God. Religious materialists believe that the truth has assumed religious form so that religion (dogma) becomes the pathway to God or salvation, and salvation itself became the major objective—the ultimate material gain.

Philosophically or reasonably, there's no other alternative to the concept of salvation by work other than justification by faith. And these two concepts couldn't be combined for their natures are the antitheses of each other, but one must be the supreme truth, and it's an individual choice and responsibility. This is the main objective of creation. Humanity is given the innate capacity of reason to exercise or reject the truth. The truth is always an individual perception through pure individual response to the stimulus of reason presented by another. Because physical life couldn't exist without freedom, as evident with motion of matter within and without itself, so is the spiritual discernment and pursuit (freedom of choice of lifestyle, philosophy, and belief). This is also evident in the struggle of the argument of democracy and communism or socialism. Even economic status must be based upon the argument of freedom to be justifiable. God's way of creation, therefore, is with absolute purpose through or by way of probabilities, seen by evolutionists as random acts. The relationship of purpose with probability are amiable rather than antithetical so that God's intent of creation is to obtain faith from his creation. However, God couldn't possibly coerce his creation to exercise faith; otherwise, it couldn't be an act of faith and the justice of God would be at risk.

To exactly understand or perceive the righteousness of God, God has inherently installed in humanity the capacity of reason or intellectual capability along with the ability of self-realization or understanding one's nature. Undoubtedly, physics and human sciences, as well as metaphysics or even the highest attainment of human philosophy, has gained tremendous achievements but nothing that could lead or create immortality. If humanity itself assumed the task and responsibility of achieving the condition of immortal existence, knowing the magnitude of such a proposition must be universal (if it's possible even just to know the exact size of universal matter), if it's an absolute truth that the limit of scientific technology could possibly see (according to the light it receives) the edge of the universe. And even if it did how could it possibly confirm that there's only one universe—or is it conceivable to believe that all existing light must be predestined to reach the human eye? Perhaps with the consideration of the non-physical possibility of conscious existence. If one of the preceding suppositions is probable, then the nature of absolute truth must be in the form of knowledge or science, and in religion, righteousness by works is the supreme principle of salvation.

However, as long as the concept of the existence of God is collateral with absolute incorruptible righteousness, then righteousness by works could never attend the highest argument of purity. If salvation and righteousness is a concrete, prescribed set of rules of law and liturgy, and whether such law and liturgy came from God or are the demands of God, then where's the argument and the validity of the concept of pure freedom and choice? And such a demand, if God really demands, must come directly from God himself because of the argument of the validity of pure honesty; otherwise, a human is just following another human. The biblical theology had presented physical evidence of such a God through its history; however, in this regard, the present must judge or coincide with historical claims of events (miracles) to avoid dilemma. But the condition to please and appease the demand of the direct affinity of the past with the present is not available.

The argument of the nature of the message of justification by faith in this study (Christism), although it has some relevance with the biblical theology, has also a major diversion. In this study the meaning of the message of justification by faith extends as the theory of the absolute righteousness of God correlating with the intent of creation. The act of creation must be absolutely just and righteous that reflect the justice and pure righteousness of God that couldn't possibly be corrupted. As has been previously mentioned in this study, righteousness by works has a complete attachment or derivation with the instinct of self-preservation both of the subjects of religion and religious hierarchy; the concept of righteousness by works became attributed as God's righteousness so that even the New Testament biblical theology failed to completely understand the purity of the righteousness of God. Biblical theology speculated that God demand "if you love me keep my commandment" is a very popular New Testament Scripture passage that exposed the failure of the New Testament theology to recognize the purity of the message of justification by faith.

Righteousness by works is only relevant to the horizontal human-to-human relationship, while righteousness by faith is a vertical human relationship to God which is a relationship that doesn't have preconditions, conditions, sacrifices, offerings, or whatever but a pure honest faith. Only pure and honest faith that is necessary to establish a relationship with God. Offerings and sacrifices could be offered to God but not with the concept that God demanded them for salvation or in any cause. Naturally human righteousness demands from his fellow human being under the relevance of the instinct of self-preservation, and such action is an acceptable transaction. If God, therefore, also demands (for salvation), then God's righteousness is not distinct from human righteousness. But because God doesn't demand his righteousness is pure, holy, and just, this idea of the righteousness of God poses a great dilemma with the religious materialist whose main concern is power and economic benefit. Apostle Paul came very close to complete understanding of the message of justification by faith so that he found struggles of his human nature (Romans Chapter 7) when he had partially seen the pure righteousness of God. The problem with the biblical message of justification by faith is that they tried to unite the message of righteousness by works as expressed with passages or scriptures like: "If you love me keep my commandments" and "I'll show you my faith by my works." Regardless that the biblical Christ reconciled man by himself unto himself, the same Christ issued demands: "If you love me keep my commandments" and "Be ye therefore perfect even as your father which is in heaven is perfect" (Matthew 5:48). Even Apostle Paul expressed the demand of God (Romans 6:13) or Christ for example in his book Ephesians (Ephesians 4: 12; 5:10; 20, 21, 24, 27) as the union of Christ and Church almost became indistinguishable; in fact, the Church received recognition as the body of Christ.

Although Apostle Paul seemed revolutionary with his presentation of the message of justification by faith, he is only halfway to understanding the ultimate message of justification by faith. How? (Romans 3:31). Apostle Paul attributed that the Ten Commandments, as well as the other commandments, are absolute demands of God, but he failed to recognize that as long as any law or commandment is being fulfilled or observed as the demand of God, there is no clear distinction between righteousness by faith and righteousness by works.

As previously recognized or presented on many occasions in this study, if God demands, then his righteousness couldn't possibly attend absolute purity and incorruptibility. And the order by which to understand the purity of the righteousness of God is to completely separate the concept of righteousness by faith from righteousness by work, through the study of the mechanism and nature of creation. Because the whole creation is the expression of the righteousness of God by which the hath inherently given to us as the structure of morality (see Structure of Morality), it's imperative to understand the absolute righteousness of God, not only for the attainment of the absolute truth of theosophy or philosophical reasoning of existence but also to appreciate the beauty of the act of creation by God, regardless of the presence of mortality. To be able to completely separate the concept of justification by faith from righteousness by work, one of the major stipulations to be brought about is the very fact that any individual is capable of performing good moral acts without the knowledge or faith of the existence of God. In simple analysis, faith doesn't preempt or preclude nonbelievers/atheists from the exercise of good works. And good works is not to be exclusively definitive, according to religious forms. In fact, all organisms are capable of good works according to each species' requirements or considerations. Righteousness by works, therefore, is an absolute part of the plan of creation which is evident in the structure of morality level 1 and 2, and level 3 is the transitionary event that prepared the creation of human beings with the capability to accept or reject faith. According to the structure of morality presented in this study, the exercise of righteousness by work is confined from level 1 to level 3, and the rest is considered under the realm of faith. it's evident that the exercise and performance of level 1 to level 3 of the structure of morality has always been possible without faith or the belief of the existence of God. Although, the exercise of righteousness by works is absolutely available to all, it's also relative to freedom of choice so that every individual has the capacity to violate/deny each part of the structure of morality. For example, if an individual denies self preservation then the commission or act of self destruction is the result, and so is the rest of the structure of morality if improperly executed (imbalance) is the result of all the sins conceivable to existence (as stipulated in this study). Therefore, the proper balance/execution of the level 1 to level 3 of the structure of morality will sustain an orderly society even without the belief or faith of the existence of God.

So far, it's evident that righteousness by works is completely separable from righteousness by faith, and one is not a condition or precondition of the other because God in his absolute righteousness intended it to be so. Righteousness by works, therefore, must only be with relevance as a horizontal relationship between man to man or human to human. It will never be between God and man. In fact, the New Testament theology of the Judeo-Christian Scripture as depicted by the Gospel event is an attempt to understand the concept. But the New Testament concept of justification by faith failed to have recognized the complete beauty of the message of justification by faith on the basis that, regardless that salvation became only possible through the Gospel or Jesus Christ, the same Jesus Christ issued the demands: Pick up your cross and follow me- and -If you love me keep my commandments" and "Blessed are they..." (see Sermon on the Mount), etc. Actually. the Gospel concept of the New Testament theology event removed ("by the deeds of the law no man is justified before God") all the requirements (moral or ceremonial) for salvation; all the works of Jesus Christ became irrelevant on the fact that the same Jesus issued demands for salvation. Therefore, the Gospel event is only a half-way understanding of the pure absolute message of justification by faith of the righteousness of God, because the Gospel is only an artificial mediatorship—which means nothing because if God demands, then faith in God is the absolute precondition of good works and humanity must be a moral robot of God—referred to in this study as a condition of robotic moralism. The Judeo-Christian understanding of the message of justification by faith culminated in self-destruction, taking all things into consideration.

To explore or elucidate further the Pauline message of justification by faith. in Romans 3:21; 2:9-11; and 15:16-29 it's evident that salvation is no longer proprietary or for the Jews only. Because the Gospel fulfilled the ceremonial (that the law demands death for salvation) law aspect of salvation, the Jewish religion no longer had any difference even with the Gentiles who don't believe God. The fact that the Gentiles or unbelievers also could perform moral conduct even outside the concept of the existence of God, which means that the Gentiles also know how to love oneself (self-preservation), offspring, relatives, friends, government, nature, art, etc. Because the difference between the Jews and the Gentiles is only the ceremonial law or the concept of sanctuary for salvation and when the sanctuary concept was abolished the difference was eliminated, if the Gentile is convinced to offer good works to God by believing with the Gospel, then salvation is warranted. Because the Gospel limited (moral law) its demand for salvation, salvation became universally available for all, and no longer for the Jews only but also to the Gentiles. But even if the Gospel fulfilled all the laws for human salvation, the same Gospel still demanded the observance of the moral law: "If you love me keep my commandments" (mentality).

The Judeo-Christian theology will always remain ambiguous with its theory of salvation—as it has been the major debate and argument of religious scholars—and there will never be a clear presentation of the message of justification by faith as long as the Holy Bible is regarded as the only fundamental basis of truth for the very reason that the Judeo-Christian biblical theology couldn't completely separate the concept of righteousness by work from righteousness by faith. The major failure, perhaps of all religious concepts, in on the basis of their deficiency to recognize the human nature with inherent twofold responsibilities: first, the responsibility to self (self-preservation) and to others; second the responsibility of (faith) to God. The first human responsibility is called righteousness by works, and its' fundamental necessity if for (temporary) material existence. The second human responsibility is called faith, and its fundamental necessity is for salvation (immortality). Because all religious concepts give offerings to God, they thought that the nature of God is like human beings, it's a very common practice of religions to offer money, dance, rituals, food, animal and even human sacrifices (male or female). But even if the Judeo-Christian religion referred to in this study as the most sophisticated religion of Earth because of its theology of the Gospel or justification by faith which thought it had recognized the futility of sacrifices, instead sacrificed their God for their salvation. But even if the Gospel retained the observance of the moral codes—love thy neighbor as thy self—the object of moral codes could not be mere idealism because it's impossible to love yourself (or your starving neighbor) without fulfilling its material (foods, etc.) demands.

The New Testament Judeo-Christian theology became the love of others and the Church. Thy neighbor and the Church became the Christ (read the book of Ephesians 1:22-23; 2:20-22; 5:23-32). Any religious concept that holds the notion that God demands the principle "love thy neighbor as thy self" as a duty to God or part of faith will violate the logic of absolute truth or the pure message of justification by faith. The only responsibility or duty of man to his God is only pure and honest faith or to believe in God, and the same God only demands faith (spiritual or immaterial). In fact, such faith is not even a demand of God but is already in us for humanity to recognize through the eye of reason or wisdom. Also, the need of righteousness by works is already in every human being for it's the requirement of the very infrastructure of all material existence. Therefore, if any human being violates the first three levels of the structure of morality, he is in violation (as discussed previously or in the structure of morality) of his inherent nature with respect to his relationship to his fellow human being, and if any human being who denies his faith to God likewise violated his inherent nature with respect to his relationship to his Creator or God. Therefore, righteousness by works and righteousness by faith, since one has horizontal disbursement and the other has a vertical allocation, are completely without demand from one to another. Man, therefore, has to completely see and treat God as God through faith and a fellow man as a man, a man with needs.

Any religious concept which disregards complete separation of righteousness by work from righteousness by faith violates the principle of freedom, justice of God, and the act or nature of creation. All organisms which have no capability of faith in God could perform righteousness by works and even an atheist human could exceed the righteousness by works of human beings having faith in God. The justice and righteousness of God's act of creation must be seen in the manner that faith in God must be completely acquired individual freedom of choice, not being coerced by its inherent nature of material survival. Therefore, the material and spiritual, although they are one, they are completely separate. This is the mystery of creation that the spirit of God and man in man is in the human flesh. The trinitarian concept of creation is the human flesh created by God the father (nothing or void), and the son of God (matter) created the human spirit. And the human spirit unknowingly used the spirit of God, so that when a human dies, the Holy Spirit returns to God with the record of how it was used; therefore, God knew who violated the structure of morality. It is a very important issue to understand that the full compliance of the structure of morality (work and faith) couldn't be a demand of God for the very reason that it's a human responsibility. Because if God demands, he couldn't have incorruptible righteousness, and it could suggest that man is superior to God intelligence.

If God utilizes (without demand) criteria of salvation according to the concept of the observance of the complete separation of righteousness by work and righteousness (justification) by faith, then atheists who had no faith in God and believers in God who only perform good works according to a command or demand and the prospect of salvation, couldn't possibly obtain salvation. In this study of Christism, it became obvious that God doesn't demand for salvation. Because if the atheist is inherently capable of good works without faith in God, then the assertion of the book of James Chapter 2 by Apostle James became irrelevant, not only of the preceding arguments, but also because faith is inherently provided in human beings that it could be denied or accepted. The big question of Apostle James is whether it's possible to have faith in God and one could completely deny performing good works concurrently. Perhaps Apostle James didn't really see the irrelevant nature of his inquiry. Perhaps he either denied or ignored for some reason the fact that even the Gentiles (non-believers in God) are inherently capable of moral virtue of loving oneself and others. And even further, Apostle James failed to understand that faith in God is exclusively a personal relationship with God, regardless of membership to any religious congregation, so that only the individual and God really know the degree and sincerity of one's faith. So, if any man demands the exhibition of one's faith to God by the performance of good works, it is a pure violation of freedom, and it could mean a moral extortion. God couldn't be a moral extortionist because human beings were not created as moral robots.

Although Apostle James and Paul have a different approach of how to obtain salvation, both of them failed to completely understand the absolute truth. Apostle James failed to recognize the necessity for complete separation of righteousness by work from justification by faith by fusing them together (James Chapter 2). On the other hand, Apostle Paul's methodology used the Gospel (Christ) to demand the observance of the moral codes, while completely (correctly) demolishing the observance of all ceremonial laws by the Gospel or Christ who, regardless that he became the substance of faith, has no major impact to the procurement of absolute truth for the fundamental concept that the purpose of demand remains unchanged, regardless of ways and means.

Throughout the human historical past, it's completely apparent that human beings regarded God as a very demanding creator. Throughout the ages of history, we found all religious concepts performing acts of offering: words, deeds, or corporeal sacrificial offerings (including human beings) just to please God. However, fortunately, the beginning of the understanding of absolute truth began to unravel, particularly with the concept of Apostle Paul, which is mostly written in his epistles to the Romans. And because of the inclusiveness of this theory, all religious concepts or beliefs are reconcilable to God. Apostle Paul laid the foundation of the understanding of absolute truth, regardless that it is incomplete or imperfect, it doesn't mean that he labored in vain because it's in his sincerity to the quest of the final truth that would determine his eternal fate on a personal basis with his right standing before God.

It is necessary to better sharpen our understanding of the Gospel event, not only that it's the major hub of the most sophisticated religious organization that existed in this world—the Judeo-Christian faith, whether it's Catholicism or Protestantism—but also its universal grasp or implication on the search for the final truth of the highest probability of the existence of God. Because the Gospel event is by nature a quest for truth, it must be reconciled with the concept of this study.

It's evident that the Gospel event is a fulfillment of the demand of God. In a simple analysis, God reconciled man unto himself (a biblical Pauline theology). But even if the biblical Gospel didn't take place, the same God demanded, according to the Old Testament (Bible) theology with the Genesis post—creation of Adam and Eve in the Garden of Eden. The Garden of Eden debacle exposed the quest for the explanation of human sin and mortality. Therefore, mortality became a demand of God for retribution of sin by which the same theory ultimately culminated with the New Testament Gospel event by which became the only hope of reconciliation for salvation—the God who reconciled man unto himself concept (11 Cor. 5:18) for the very reason that no human sacrifices, offerings, deeds, or worship could appease God's demand for humanity transgression of his law. It seems, therefore, that the Gospel event (according to the Bible) itself is an outright exposition of the severity that God is hard to please: that he alone can please himself because every human being is sinful. The concept of sinful predisposition (Rom. 3:23 "For all have sinned and come short of the glory of God") preceded the study of genetics by a priest, Gregor Mendel.

As far as the biblical or Judeo-Christian concept, the righteousness of God is based solely on the idea that God demands, written in the form of moral and ceremonial laws. And the Gospel event abolished all ceremonial laws but retained all moral laws as a precondition of salvation.

166

Unfortunately, the love of God and fellow man is written in one table of code called the Ten Commandments.

But the Bible of the Judeo-Christian theology to be praised with its Pauline concept of justification by faith. It's a very simple method to reconcile Apostle Paul's theory of justification by faith with this (Christism concept) study. Apostle Paul's most insightful concept is Romans 3:28: "Therefore we conclude that a man is justified by faith without the deeds of the law." This is an expression of pure, unadulterated faith, but in the next verse, Romans 3:31, Apostle Paul tries to reconcile the dilemma: "Do we then make void of the law through faith? God forbid: yea we stablish the law. " The only viable reconciliation of the dilemma of faith and works (obedience of the law) is for Apostle Paul to place all good works of law to the trust of the Gospel, not to merit salvation by a follower of the Lord (faith and Gospel). All the admonitions of Apostle Paul of good works, deeds, hardships, and righteousness become the outcome of faith in Jesus Christ, I Thessalonians 1:6; Colossians 3:15, 16, 17, 20, 23, 24: II Thessalonians 1:12; and Il Timothy 2:4, 15, 19, 24 are just a few incidents.

It became so obvious that the Apostle wrestled more than any other apostles or the writers of the synaptic gospel to reconcile work and faith in his books but regardless, like Apostle James, failed to recognize to obtain a pure gospel message or absolute truth. The Gospel event, therefore, completely throughout the Judeo-Christian biblical theology, became the fusion of righteousness by works and faith on the basis that Jesus Christ demanded the continual observance of moral laws for salvation, and on one side abolished fulfilling the demand of the law of sacrificial offering with blood or death. In simple analysis, the meaning of faith is unilaterally attributed to the concept that the demand (capital corporeal punishment) for the satisfaction of the broken law of God was given complete fulfillment by the Calvary event. To the biblical theology or theosophy, the Gospel therefore became the embodiment of the final truth: the concept of I am the way, the truth, and the life.

But suppose that there wasn't really a Jesus Christ in person that existed, but only as the exemplified embodiment of the search for the truth. What if the Cosmic Christ, according to this study so that the presence of the process of the search of the absolute incorruptible truth, is one of the very pieces of evidence that God exists, and such an understanding of an absolute incorruptible truth is the only viable way to usher in the immortal coming dimension of reality?

It's already been presented on more than one occasion that it's only on the condition that God doesn't demand for salvation, by the method of the complete separation of the concept of righteousness by works and righteousness by faith that the absolute incorruptible truth could be understood and derived. Since all religious concepts that so far existed by one way or another have understood that God demands for salvation, the Judeo-Christian theology has the most sophisticated form by the token of the Gospel event that abolished the most horrible demand of God: capital corporeal punishment by death. Unfortunately, even to the present era of human governments, the concept of the death sentence is readily practiced and even adored as a form of capital corporeal punishment, and surprisingly enough, it's a popular demand and advocated among religious political groups.

The Judeo-Christian Gospel is not only a form of reconciliation of the relationship of law and faith and/or punishment and forgiveness, but also epitomized the historical struggle of the search of the truth of the nature of existence as evidence of the theological exposition of biblical concepts of Genesis to the Book of Revelation, which revealed its opinion about creation, sin, mortality, reconciliation, forgiveness, salvation, and immortality. Regardless of the tremendous advances of science and philosophy, the biblical concept of truth via the Gospel event shouldn't be completely dishonored, even if its proponents could be more often than not outrightly arrogant to regard it as a complete and final absolute truth, not only for themselves but also to imposing it on their fellow human beings as indicative of what has become of the continuing destruction of individual liberty.

In this study with all its accommodations and kindnesses to the Christian Gospel, this study has offered a compromise. The objective and goal of this study is not committed with the task of the destruction of the Christian Gospel but to the most honest pursuit of the truth, and by no means with any reservations but with full compliance to the concept of freedom.

There's only one way for all religious forms and concepts to be reconciled to the justice and absolute righteousness of God: by the method of what has been proposed in this study, of the observance of the complete separation of righteousness by work and justification by faith so that all religious practices of benign offerings of any sorts could remain to be offered only by virtue as a voluntary *expression of gratitude to God*, which is not by any means demanded by God for any purposes of salvation and also for life to be well sustained and balanced.

The preceding arguments are the most viable procedures for wisdom or knowledge to see the ultimate incorruptibility of the righteousness of a Divine Creator. It's the only alternative to the failure of history. Shall we discard the New Testament Gospel? Absolutely not, because of its courageous initiative of the message of justification by faith regardless that it's rudimentary and faulty, but the concern and interest for the search of a better if not absolute truth is conspicuous.

The fact must be faced boldly that righteousness by works, as evidence of the love of self and others, is an inherent, integral part of the plan of creation, otherwise, creation couldn't sustain itself, and in like manner, so with the concept of faith. The structure of morality, as has been presented in this study, although is has a common origin, the two parts aren't completely integral, and although complementary, they are completely separate. It's relativity synchronous with the nature of universal existence that God the father (the nothing or void) and God the Son (the matter or energy) are one in purpose and complementary

169

as the only means to sustain all creation. Regardless, one has its own separate life, personality, identity, or spirit and yet couldn't exist without the other even in terms of having a life of its own.

Truth is not empty idealism, so an individual who professes to have faith in God and denies the truth to his fellow man is as immature as to demand another's individual evidence of faith. it's the purpose of the creator to have provided humanity with great wisdom to avoid the dilemma of the ignorance of self-realization for the purpose of the production of freedom and responsibility. The concept to demand God to demand responsibility for salvation from human beings is outright ignorance of the truth, thereby is the source of the production of robotic moralism. It is the source and interest of bold legalists and religious materialists.

Truth also is not unilateral materialism, but it's the acknowledgment for the existence of God the father (the void) and God the Son (the matter); likewise, truth is not unilateral spiritualism, for there's no known existence of knowledge and wisdom outside matter. Even God the father must interact with God the son to sustain its spirit and life. The concept of the probability of the existence of spirit outside matter or flesh couldn't be sustained for the very reason that matter has existed and is best exemplified by human existence. There must be a logical purpose of life of the consciousness of matter, isn't there?

All truth, therefore, must be argued and derived upon the nature of universal existence so that there's no possibility that the universe consists of matter alone, tangible or intangible, because truth is logic and reason so that the proposition of the existence of intangible matter is a deceptive argument on the basis that matter must be physically verifiable, and anything that could not be physically verified is void or nothing. If nothing or void could be verified, then how far is infinity? Could infinity be verified or measured? No, it couldn't, just as how energy came into being couldn't be verified and yet it's definitely matter. Reason, therefore, couldn't accept the logic of unilateral materialism because the question about infinity couldn't be answered mutually as the question of how energy came into being.

On the basis that there's no sole authentic scientific explanation of the origin of all things/matter/void which could ever be derived or be probable, faith is more an easy process of acknowledgment of the existence of a creator. Faith is also a struggle of constant vigilance, similarly with the responsibility to oneself and to others. It is completely obvious that the instinct of self-preservation is present in all organisms; otherwise, creation has no purpose and couldn't have happened. Purpose, therefore, has preexistence before creation. It's impossible to believe that the first organism could have survived without the instinct to survive or to eat. The instinct of self-preservation or the love of oneself is not a demand from God but a condition for survival freely given by creator and always at the direct discretion of individual freedom. Therefore, the concept that the love of oneself, others, and God is a demand by God for salvation, and such a demand is the sole purpose of individual purpose to live and act, is a condition of robotic moralism. Humanity's perception of reality negated the fact that creation couldn't have taken place without the structure of morality. It's impossible. Otherwise, God completely had a child's play of rolling the dice and just waited for probabilities until an organism acquired survival instincts. The structure of morality, therefore, was and is a condition of creation and existence and aren't demands for the concept of salvation.

The logic of demand destroys honesty and freedom. Demand is corruptible, while obligation is incorruptible. The absolute righteousness of God, therefore, is dependent with the completion of obligations and the absence of demand. Demand is a concept of moral management which is not relevant to the concept of paradise. As estate of paradise is not a convergence of engineering and management expertise: regardless, immortality or salvation must be a structural part of the nature of creation or existence. Because it's only God the creator who could possibly issue the estate of immortality and obligation and is the only source of righteousness; otherwise, if man is entrusted with the duty to provide himself immortality, then the management of demand or robotic morality would be the ruler of society.

It's apparent that the Judeo-Christian theology of the Old Testament Bible exemplified a classical state of fulfillment of demands as the precept for salvation or righteousness on both interactions of vertical and horizontal human existence. Even the New Testament theology wasn't spare the same dilemma so that the Gospel event was just an attempt that came close to the understanding of the absolute truth of the purity of the righteousness of God as has been stipulated and revealed in this study.

If one's perception of truth doesn't deviate from the theology of the Judeo=Christian Bible, the perception about the nature of existence of what is called "Heaven" or "Paradise" would be an estate of the state of situation of moral management, therefore, there will be governments. But this condition is a complete misunderstanding of a basic logic. Why moral management when immortality already exists? Has not the sin problem been completely dealt with? Do we make the creator an idiot?

It sufficeth to confirm that the Judeo-Christian concepts of heaven and original sin are the result of the non-fulfillment and fulfillment of the demand(s) of God, considered as the commandments of God, so that the concept of immortality is retrievable by God rather than granted as a one-time event. But immortality must be irretrievable as a more viable logic that could issue relevance to the superior intelligence of a creator. If immortality is retrievable, then the provider (God) lacks anticipation of the future, and if immortality is retrievable, the switch form one condition to another is a situation never attempted to be explained even by Judeo-Christian Scripture itself. The physiological and anatomical consideration before the immortal body of Adam and Eve, the argument of bodily injury (even disregarding the argument of immunity against pathogens) requires heavy philosophical and physical reconciliation to be believable. But the underlying argument of why Adam and Eve were stripped of immortality is on the basis of the same argument of the fall of

Lucifer from heaven. The fall of Lucifer postulated by biblical arguments sufficed to indicate a power structure or hierarchy that allegedly existed in heaven. But that procedure or line of argument is faulty; regardless, the biblical theology must retain coherence of its own assertion of an opinion system to at least look or appear truthful. If in heavenly places where Lucifer came from there exists a power structure, it's only logical to believe that being righteous is being in conformity with existing demands or laws of God.

According to biblical assertions, it's therefore apparent that laws and demands of God has existed before (or during) and after immortality. This biblical concept of humanity's destiny of the restoration or proposition or belief system of heaven or paradise has retained the same argument. But contrary to this study, any immortal dimension or state of reality doesn't require any form of government or power structure for the administration of laws for the very reason and purpose that there would be no existence of demand and law. It's illogical to believe that in an immortal existence the possibility of sin could still exist regardless that the knowledge of right and wrong is available. What sinful act could be useful or beneficial in an immortal dimension? And who desires for heaven only for the purpose of power and selfishness?

In Figure 1, the relationship of faith and work is illustrated as separate but one, one through the outworking of the Holy Spirit of God by way of 1) reason, 2) understanding the nature of existence both local and universal, and 3) through special revelations (individual personal life mystical experiences). This way is evident as humanity found his God and faith as explained in this study. The very nature of the universe and nature of life (notunol) is itself the methodology of God's election for salvation.

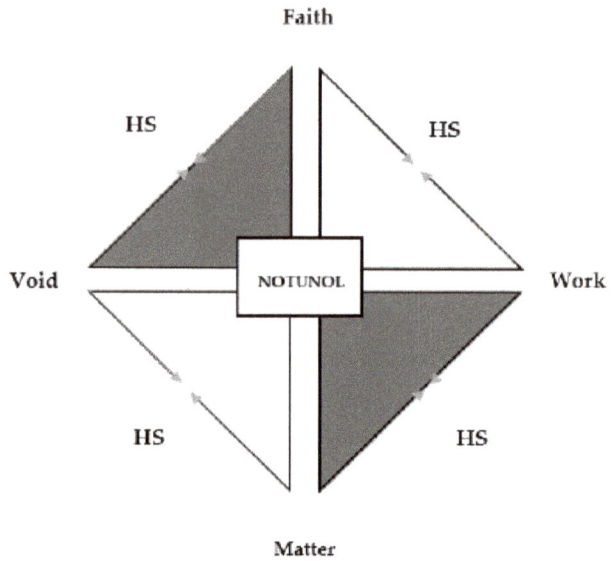

Faith

HS

HS

Void

NOTUNOL

Work

HS

HS

Matter

Election by Faith for Salvation

Fig. 1

Legend: HS = Holy Spirit

In the same Figure 1, the relationship between void (God the father) and matter (God the son) is also illustrated as separate but one in purpose and spirit. But the relationship of faith and God the father (void—as the primary cause and object of faith) are inseparable, and one as indicated by the dark color. And the deity knew beforehand that true faith will begat true works and the beneficiary of works is the matter (life) itself so that works, and matter are inseparable, and one as indicated by dark color. Figure 1, therefore, has illustrated the unified nature of existence. But because of the interrelationship outworking of the Holy

Spirit of God, many become confused or unclear on many major issues of existence, for instance, regarding how many varied religious (separatist) concepts had evolved, also how various forms of unilateral materialism and spiritualism have misconstrued the basic relationship of matter and void and/or God the father and son. But especially how the relationship of faith and works that has been misunderstood by many and if not all religious concepts. All of these major problems of existence have been given reconciliations and explanations in this study.

The Dilemma of Present Era Stern and
Excessive Moral Management

It has been stipulated in this study that the hub of all life freedom and conscience (*conscience*: defined as knowing right from wrong). Without it, universal existence, moral or physical, is not possible. The presence of freedom and conscience given to man epitomize the absolute righteousness of God, and when the absolute righteousness and nature of God is fully understood, it will serve as the hub of true faith that brings forth voluntary righteousness of work.

By religion. the root and cause of all the destructions of individual liberty is with the misunderstanding of the nature of the righteousness of God. Leaders and organizational geniuses seem to forget that it's only on the basis of the probability that righteousness could exist, and it is of the evidence that could support the concept that God really does exist. If God exists, He must therefore possess righteousness. God couldn't in any way possibly be partially evil, could the devil in any way possibly be partially righteous. And only because God has absolute righteousness is the very logical deduction that God does exist and an absolute evil (personally physical or spiritual [physically unseen] in nature) couldn't possibly exist. And any stipulation that the existence and embodiment of evil is the void, or nothing is complete idiocy. Christianity, and not all present religious concepts, has to defend the concept of the existence of evil/devil so that there's and existence of God; if God exists then evil must also exist. Since the Judeo-Christian Bible has declared itself as "the word of God," it's a very enigmatic situation for them to abandon the idea of the existence of evil. All Christians who adhere to the principle of the absolute verity of the Bible have no other option but to defend the concept of the existence of a physical or spiritual (unseen) embodiment of the devil. Christianity must maintain a faith of the existence of the physical devil; otherwise, its whole theology will collapse. But when the question is asked of why the Christ and devil disappeared at the same time in human history, what answer could be given? Did Christ take the devil with him in heaven? In fact, there were only two major appearances of physical evil in the Bible: first, as a serpent tempting Eve in the Garden of Eden in the book of Genesis: second, tempting Jesus Christ in the New Testament (Matthew 4:1-11). Therefore, if there is no actual personal or spirit existence of a devil, then Christianity and all the rest of the cluster of religious concepts who believe in the existence of physical or spiritual embodiment of a devil will forever be doomed to committing a major falsehood—so that falsehood begat falsehood, it seems—becoming the only recourse to protect the truth for them. And it will always be a problematic situation when faith is absolutely attributed to mere idealism and dogma rather than the other way: that human detrimental/destructive behavior is evil as the violation of the structure of morality given by the creator, but not that human detrimental/destructive behavior is being inspired by an alleged existence of a devil. Christianity, therefore, and all the rest of the religious concepts who believe in the existence (personal or spirit) of a devil must carry the dilemma to prove its truthfulness—and in reality, only movies are filled with them.

It must be taken into consideration that even the existence of Christ presented by the Bible could easily be disproven by a simple honest inquiry of reason. And how much more enigmatic is probing the truth of whether the existence of the biblical Christ must be in conjunction with the existence of the devil; is it, therefore, only a matter of an argument of coincidence that both disappeared at the same time from humanity's historical past? Or is it just a matter of a failure of systematic theology? What logical disadvantage is there if the devil shows its presence? And what logical advantage is there if the devil doesn't show its presence?

It's supposed to be undeniably illogical to impose a strict unnecessary moral code of conduct upon ordinary human beings or to the whole wide world's inhabitants, because the prime enemy of the Church and/or government is considered to be the devil itself, which presence cannot be presently absolutely substantiated. And even the devil worshippers themselves hadn't seen the embodiment of their master. In fact, modern concepts seemed to suggest that individual freedom is becoming attributed more to the personality of the devil, and it seems to be becoming a more appealing concept to live (with toil) in hell with freedom than morally incarcerated in heaven which might be full of gold and silver. It's not hard to believe that the present humanity remains not fighting the real battle. And if there would be a real culprit to the dilemma, it would be with the fundamental error that man assumed an absolute truth either by himself to himself or allegedly given by God. It's promulgated on this study, by this study, that this study must not be imposed as an absolute truth but rather as an honest search of the absolute truth whether or not there is a participation of God, invoked or uninvoked, because faith is yet to be glorified when the immortal dimension becomes the overriding reality. This is the essence of faith, and so the process of the absolute honest election for immortality wouldn't be jeopardized.

Let us allow a little illustration as to why there's no absolute with human perception or ideology (read also The Truth and Mathematics). Let us ask the question: does anybody have the freedom to kill anybody? Of course, our hands aren't tied together, but (relative to one action) one must also be willing to admit the freedom to be killed. Therefore, the applications of freedom are relative and not absolute (it's the very reason that freedom is a co-function of conscience, and one couldn't exist or is irrelevant without the other (read Structure of Morality). However, it's the need and availability of freedom that is absolute, which is given by the creator.

Because there's no absolute in humanity, the management of morality must be limited and must be confined to the immediate purpose of the preservation of life because the intent of God's creation is life. Let's take the discussion of freedom in another position. The imposition of the mandatory school uniform almost became a worldwide proportion. This issue has pushed humanity to the level of non-rational beings, like plants and animals or even inanimate objects. It's in fact, a direct violation of the nature of creation (by God, if you will). Whether we like it or not, this issue is nothing but a conditioned reflex of unnecessary moral management which benefits nothing but materialism and authoritarianism.

Let's sharpen the discussion a little further with the most famous controversial prohibition against sexual prostitution. Prostitution is being perceived by many under the name of morality as immoral. In fact, it's the prohibition that is immoral. Without prostitution there's no mechanism to issue relevance to the honesty of the institution of marriage; and prostitution serves as an alternative to solving the issue of the imbalance of the ratio of male and female; and as a resort for those who perceive or regard that masturbation (although being taught generally as normal) is more immoral than sexual engagement with prostitutes; and for those who couldn't afford what has become the rigorous and expensive conditions of marital life in modern society, even disregarding what has evolved of the social pattern of the sophisticated maze and heavily cultured requirements of courtship.

The aforementioned are just a couple of examples of an excessive intrusion into the innocuous individual liberty by the majority of society, religion, and government. And the underpinning and most basic cause remains the same: the misunderstanding of the nature and/or righteousness of our creator.

But even if the argument would be considered on the lower level of contention outside the consideration of the existence of a creator, still the necessity of the existence of freedom remains absolute for the fact that no honest, valid understanding or perception of morality or moral values could be derived without it. Perhaps one of the grievous errors of unilateral materialism philosophy, like socialism or communism, is their failure of finding the real origin of human moral values. Communism as well as socialism are not void of the claim of moral values, regardless that their prime morality revolves with the equal distribution of material wealth. Because unilateral materialism traces the origin of matter from accidental episodes, likewise their perception of moral values must have come from the happenstance of the evolutionary process believed to be millions, if not billions, of years of conditioning or with what is more scholastically referred to as environmental (imposed by) adaptation. But when the question of when the first organism(s) or life form(s) obtained its/their first adapted instincts of survival, the answer is not available. And what period of time did it take for the first instinct of survival (desire to survive) to come about? The basic concept of $r=c/p$ must also apply to dispute the evolutionist theory, that the first creature(s), whatever that was, originally possessed perception or intelligence; perception wasn't created by environmental circumstances, but rather intelligence adjusted itself to the variation of environmental circumstances and not the other way because any progression of evolutionary process couldn't possibly proceed without intelligence or purpose. Purpose, therefore, guided various proprietary evolutionary processes, and such a purpose is structured with morality described in the discussion of the structure of morality.

A very interesting concept could be brought about: if everything came from a mere chance, then why are communism or socialism regressive and inflexible against individual liberty? Why be rigid with human rights and every little innocuous individual liberty? After all, there is no purpose from the beginning of life. So, the dilemma for excessive authority, whether it be under communism or democratic forms of governments, and at the present age it has become without much distinction. In fact, in some instances democratic forms of government are becoming more tyrannical or oppressive than its socialist/communist counterparts, especially against innocuous individual liberties.

But for further discussion, forget communism or unilateral materialism altogether because it has denied itself the chance for eternal life; however, with any democratic government which by itself, regardless that it couldn't possibly completely separate itself from religion, its dilemma, or why it became oppressive against individual liberty, is with its fundamental error of its understanding of the nature of the gods or God's creation.

There are only two ways upon which is absolute righteousness of God could be perceived or understood. But only one could be the correct rendition:

    a.   Absolute power/righteousness by work

    b.   Absolute humility/righteousness by faith

Most, if not all religious concepts promote the idea that the gods absolutely demand worship. This is the basis of all the creations of religious laws, demands, and the offerings of sacrifices. Religious schools of thought perpetuated the notion that worship to God as not only the primary reason of creation but also for salvation (John 4:20-24; Revelation 2:2-9; Revelation 4:10; Revelation 15:4; Acts 24:14; Matthew 19:16, 21). If God absolutely demands worship, then the gods also must have demanded absolute control of human mentality and morality.

The occurrence of sin—its origin is as mysterious as the origin of life itself—seems to have been neglected of its major implications of the intent of God's way of creation. If God absolutely demands worship, then any form of sin couldn't have occurred. Man is becoming more sinful only because more and more laws are being instituted, mostly against all fronts of human activities and behavior. And if the trend will continue, human reason—the overall mental faculty—will eventually become the major casualty, and human beings will ultimately turn into an absolute robotic subject by authoritarianism garb under the name of democracy, morality, or what have they.

It is an imperative issue to be addressed of what would be the final destiny of humanity. Will the majority of human beings ultimately become mechanical robots by the managers of society forever? Or will the immortal dimension of reality eventually take over wherein any form of government or social managers don't exist? In the present era of both government and religion, it only seems that the intrusion/infringement of excessive unnecessary laws and futile mediums of moral control into individual liberty is at its highest proportion.

It's the intent of this study to provide comfort and mechanism to an honest individual seeking the absolute truth to alleviate his/her suffering from the unduly or cruel restrictions of individual liberty. The author of this study believes that an immortal dimension of reality without any form of government will someday come into reality, a reality or state of life where self-governance will maintain social order. Any human being who would have access to this study must be clearly informed of self-governance and discipline in anticipation of the coming immortal reality. Even if this modality of life is not possible with the present dispensation, the desire and anticipation of its reality might usher in or hasten the coming of the immortal dimension yet to come, to cut short the suffering of the righteous people of God.

Even the Christian Scripture had vividly portrayed, perhaps even to the highest clarity, the absolute humility of the Savior Jesus Christ on Mount Calvary a sacrifice of one's life for the redemption of humanity's sins and which in theology (in religion) became the message of justification by faith. And even if the Jesus Christ event didn't really take place (literally), it has no major significance to the search of absolute truth because it's the portrayal of the absolute character of God that is the issue. And whoever or whatever the embodiment of God is, the truth must be conveyed and understood.

181

The greatest failure of the leaders of today's society is in the fundamental misunderstanding of the nature of God's/gods' righteousness and the nature of creation in general; most if not all leaders (moral or physical, religious or scientific) assumed to themselves the possession of absolute truth. This is the major, if not the sole, causation of all unduly oppressive intrusions into individual liberty. Today's leaders seem to forget the fundamental fact that even the actual nature and origin of energy remains beyond the grasp of human intelligence. And how much more could humanity understand the infinite nature of the void or nothing/ space? It's not because human intelligence becoming capable of measuring and manipulating various forms of energy is a sufficient understanding of the nature of all things, and relatively speaking, humans remained disappointed in finding the cure of humanity's mortality.

Unless humanity should accept the fact that faith is the only major purpose of creation, and it is the only viable path for understanding the nature of God's righteousness and universal creation in general. The object of faith, as well as how it must be honestly derived, should be the major modality of all bases of morality or truth, and the only precursor to the full understanding of this concept is through freedom and conscience as the third part of the structure of morality. Without the third structure of morality, faith couldn't be possible, and creation should have been perfect and immortal form the beginning and the possibility of sin could not have been available, but universal existence itself may not have progressed as it is now. Even the theory of general relativity understood the concept of freedom according to the nature of energy it has postulated and also embraced by the theory of black hole as the absolute absence of it. This concept emphasizes that God is very much compromising of the application of the exercise of freedom.

True faith, therefore, would never be the result of moral managements; otherwise it is no faith at all, not only that the primary basis of faith is unseen, its objective worship (to Christ/or the universe) is never a demand, but rather as an obligation which resulted from self-realization and true understanding of the nature of the righteousness of God and the very nature of existence itself. Although the actual nature of the trinitarian God would never be understood by human intellect in the present dispensation, they are very much readily conceivable and appreciated, not only that humanity is one with God but also of the unified nature of universal existence. Faith of the God the father (nothing) and faith to the immortal existence of God the son (matter and its rudimentary forms) will always remain the only viable absolute justifiable (pure and honest) medium upon which the blessing of immortality would be granted.

In the present age, unfortunately, humanity remains in denial or perhaps is incapable of understanding the real message of justification by faith. It's indeed a huge dilemma for the fact that even the Christian biblical theology, regardless that is has initiated the concept of justification by faith, has failed to grasp the major profound implication of the message. Most, if not all, religious concepts had failed to understand that the real sanctuary of God is actually freedom and conscience; it's the only foundation upon which individuals may have a real honest faith and hope in God for immortality. It must be fully understood that even if God really actually intended to manage faith, it's very much unlikely that he had entrusted it through the modality of the structure or hierarchy of human power. What honest credibility could be attributed to the creator's intelligence if such is the case? But God is absolutely the very intelligent creator that he had not demanded work or managed faith.

The proper stipulation and understanding of the message of justification by faith could expose all human cunning follies and covetousness, or, on the other hand, human honest piety and prudence. So that persecution or oppression could hardly be avoided against the very foundation of the sanctuary of God, and unfortunately even among the leaders of democratic governments as well as religions hadn't avoided such rigid infringements into individuals' freedoms or liberties.

Freedom and conscience are the sanctuary of God upon which the only infrastructure of morality could support the honest and sincere proliferation of true faith. In the discussion of the structure of morality, faith is tiered with hope although the substance of faith is both tangible and intangible, the substance of hope remains first completely futuristic, but would be completely tangible as absolute righteousness and immortality when the real state or condition of the coming next dimension of existence arrives.

In the present era of stem and heavy moral managements. whether they be religion, social, civic, or government. Even if the intent is moral, it's void of actual eternal moral value; it's nothing but moral cosmetic and meaningless satisfaction of the ego of intolerance. And the saddest part of the whole operation is its merchandising; it has no difference from the sixteenth century controversy on the issue or the selling of indulgences by the Catholic faith. Whether we like it or not, the present era or heavy moral management is a form of robotic moralism. And this is a major precondition of a major direction of human destiny. Humanity might now be facing the time of election or judgment for the coming of the immortal dimension of reality; otherwise, nobody would be left uninfluenced by robotic moralists. The beginning of the true understanding of the nature of existence must start now to prepare for the coming of the next dimension of reality.

In as much that religion had long promulgated its final and ultimate capacity of its ideology and theology reclused into a biblical theological nutshell, likewise, the theory of evolution has presented its arguments—so much so that the theory of general relativity had exposed the nature of the operation of energy, but not of its actual nature or origin. Likewise, the theory of the black hole, it seems, had made its judgment call or prophecy. Notwithstanding that is seem the future is dismal, the theory of the (conservation of energy) indestructibility (that energy couldn't be created or destroyed) of energy had promulgated the highest probability of the immortality of universal existence. All of these are signs and wonders of the omnipotent power of a creature.

Since it became so obvious that freedom is the sanctuary of God, and also the only viable mechanism for the proliferation of life, physical or moral, and since the sanctuary of God resides in the hearts and minds of every individual, it's the sole determinant of the nature of faith it has grown. It's the nature of one's faith that an individual would be judged. It's an absolute verity that no other human could possibly intercede for another on the day of judgment. The nature of what event(s) would take place on the judgment day would be determined by how the sanctuary of God was treated. If God could find few individuals or groups of individuals who respected the sanctuary on the judgment day this would determine what event(s) would take place for the creation of the beginning of the immortal dimension of reality.

Humanity would be risking too much of its eternal fate if we didn't allow the proliferation of honest, innocuous, and unconventional or alternative understandings of the nature of universal existence or the deity/God. It must be fully proclaimed that scientific knowledge is completely confined or limited to what is measurable or materialistic. So is the greatest religion on Earth: the Judeo-Christian faith—based solely on pure alleged or highly doubtful historical events that had no major bearing or affinity with the present era of human existence, especially in terms of the abundant miracles it claimed, except of its assertion of the message of justification by faith. A message that found deficiencies and/or faults by this study but, however, are reconciled and purified by this study in this study.

The major stipulation of truth is that God doesn't coerce the initiation of the understanding or the acquisition of absolute truth: otherwise, faith would lose its primary objective or relevancy. And what is the relevance and responsibility of an intelligent created human being, and what would be the pleasure of a creator of creating human beings? It is through self-realization that human beings could understand the truth; it's the very reason that God has given every individual his own identity and intelligence. However, divine assistance is always available and shouldn't necessarily be denied, regardless that it Is indistinct (physical methodology), its effect is very distinct. The deity therefore has at all times constantly protected the purity of how honest faith should proliferate and be honestly sustained; otherwise, the absolute righteousness of God could be jeopardized. This philosophical assertion (that God does not demand and initiate worship to Him, that God is not a selfish God, and that a human is not God's Pavlovian dog) if this study is completely absent from the Judeo-Christian belief system—and even perhaps to all religious concepts that existed on this Earth. Collaterally with this concept, it must be absolutely imperative that the power of choice or freedom must be carefully handled by any human government, but the trend is diametrical. It became without great caution of government powers to taking away innocuous individual liberty. Morality without liberty/freedom is meaningless nor could it have any profound or genuine value even outside the argument of the concept of the existence of God. Morality without freedom could only benefit all forms of unilateral materialism either religious, secular, or scientific.

The persistence of intolerance against minorities' lifestyles in today's society reflects much of the intolerance during the New Testament mentality of heavy moral managements. This is a direct result of the majority of individuals imposing absolute truth against their fellow man, especially in terms of benign and clear innocuous behavior lifestyles. Contemplate for a moment Christian moral management in Matthew 5:27-30. This Scripture violates the concept of concept of conscience and freedom. It's a crude and cruel method of instilling (unnecessary) guilt. In fact, it violates reason and is indicative that the human might rather be a robot. The argument of Matthew 5:27-30 is morally very risky and hazardous, for the reason that it proposed no distinction between a mere thought and actual action. It suggests coerced thoughts are rather committed; after all there is no distinction in terms of guilt and/or punishment. It's very distinct that a mere thought or premeditation of action could easily be abolished or revoked, which is at times just a benign process of conscience and freedom, while on the other hand, action is clearly irretrievable and could only be forgiven or chastised.

This study doesn't in any way want to suggest that we have to discard the Bible just because of its inconsistencies or blemishes, but rather we should forgive it so that more seed of tolerance might just germinate and proliferate. Humanity must remember that the Bible has a major contribution to the truth, especially with the concept of justification by faith, regardless that it has only understood it partially; it's, however, very significant to the understanding of the probability of the existence of absolute existence of an almighty creator. Because the truth couldn't alone be supported by the material things that are created but also with the proper stipulation of philosophy, particularly which is justification by faith, which revealed the absolute righteousness of God or a creator.

Humanity is now being given the chance to accept or reject the absolute truth of justification by faith. This study has presented the truth more boldly and without reservations than its biblical New Testament predecessors. The future of humanity is in humanity's own hands. We could no longer blame God for not revealing the truth. The revelation has been given since the foundation of the physical universe, but humanity has to recognize it, and it is itself a revelation of the honest nature of a just creator. This is the truth according to Christism that revealed the nature of the universe nature of life which is the nature of God himself (Notunol) and most particularly the nature of faith for salvation.

THE TRUTH AND MATHEMATICS

THE DEVELOPMENTS OF MATHEMATICS IN ALL ITS FORMS HAS GREATLY CONTRIBUTED TO human existence toward its highest or ultimate technological achievements. Mathematics was a part of the search of the nature of existence and all its inquiries including the possible existence or nonexistence of God or the creator. Two of the most fundamental mathematical expressions or arguments are the circle and right angle. Human understanding had advanced tremendously in these aspects; despite that, humanity remains denied of immortal existence. The most probable primary reason is that physical sciences continued with its path of unilateral materialism approach of interpretations of most if not all mathematical expressions. The mathematical configuration of Figure 2 tries to illustrate or bridge the connection between the immaterial origin to the microcosm and macrocosm of dynamic as the human assumed universal as well as local physical realities, The illustration may not have an added specific actual benefit in mathematics, but definitely it shows or portrays how the universe may actually operate.

In the illustration of Figure 2, line BC, AC and Angle C become irrelevant, regardless that the use of finding the area of a right triangle is a human experience, but such an experience of knowing the area of a

189

right triangle by virtue of its mathematical propositions alone become a reality in human ordinary perceptions, but it's actually nothing but an ordinary assumption, because lines BC and AC don't really exist (in the dynamic reality) especially in the innermost dynamic interpretation of physical realm of reality, regardless that the Pythagorean theorem is mathematically admissible. In the study of chemistry by which the electron of the atom controls all the fundamental chemical reactions the reality of the existence of a straight line is not possible, because the perpetual elliptical motion of the electron(s) eliminated the notion of a straight line because a straight line is only possible when the motion of an electron stops at one point and ceases to be an energy. In a cosmic perspective, it's representative of stopping time like the black hole proposition, especially if a black hole is not energy consuming.

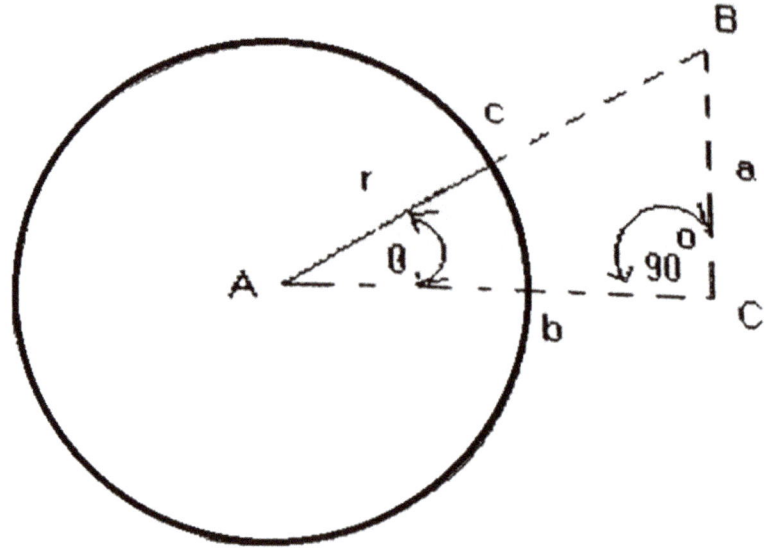

Fig. 2

In the illustration of Figure 2, line **AB** in the dynamic physical universe is actually a distance between origin (or observation-observant) point **A** and orbitant point **B** for larger domain, point **c** for smaller energy domain under consideration, so that Angle **A** has no zero (stop motion/time) value but with a 360-degree (a value mathematically assumed) rotation of motion (complete circle) because the huge primary initializing force was only a one-time event by what is referred to in this study of Christism (read Origin: Faith) as the act of creation. Line **AB** or radius **Ac**, therefore, eliminates the line **AC** in the dynamic realities where nothing is really at rest but a motion within motions (circular) of energies. There's a single proposition (although impossible) by which line **AC** could sustain itself as a straight line when an orbitant or the value of energy could reach maximum absolute zero with no energy or material force existing, likewise with line **CB** if point **B** could reach a value of infinity (or max value) and cease as an energy. But these conditions in a dynamic physical universe are not possible, as has been stipulated in Christism: only the void or nothing could assume such attributes or properties ***however, with an invisible immaterial force.*** If point **B** could reach infinity and cease to be an energy, then it's not infinite and such a proposition is inadmissible and absurdly irrelevant with the value of energy that there is no such thing as zero force in terms of energy and the existence of tiny fractions of energies don't cease to exist beyond the reckoning of human material instruments. Light radiation itself is not considered to be a straight line but a wave and particle waves must remain bearing a motion within itself (reactive) in order to be considered as a unit of energy, according to the principle of general relativity $E\text{-}mc^2$, that even the electron could gain mass when it is accelerated. It confirms that the electron continues to have a motion or energy structures within itself. The Pythagorean theorem, therefore, is only applicable in a certain domain of that which is most visible to the naked human eye perceptions and/or macrocosmic assumptive human reality and all the rest of the mathematical expressions with affinity with it.

There supposedly couldn't be any scientific theory that could support the reality of a straight line, so if space is a series of straight lines (stop and start of time/motion), then line **AB** could have a probability of reaching infinity, likewise line **AC** with an absolute zero value (with point **C** toward **A**) so that a circle is actually a straight line, and a straight line is actually a circle. If these propositions are possible, then energy could be destroyed and become completely unusable when allowed to reach beyond the domain of radius **AC** or maximum values. The proposition of a "super string" nature of space, therefore, is cataclysmic if it's intended to support the possible existence of a straight line, then non-energy-consuming black holes or otherwise are possible. Another huge proposition of a "super string" theory is that human reality could go back in time though the alleged possibility of the existence of wormholes on bended straight lines of even possibly toward the future if a wormhole in the bend of the opposite direction. On the contrary, according to the advocacy of the study of Christism, space is a void or nothing and couldn't be divided by space because it's the space (space could never be divided; its an indivisible whole with an infinite domain). The advocacy of the Pythagorean theorem, "super string," and black hole theories is a mathematical unilateral materialism interpretation of reality. The unilateral materialistic approach of mathematics is unavoidable for the fact that actual physical measurements must be undertaken to procure the value of two sides of the right triangle so that the other unknown sides or angles could be found. Even the constant value of a circle was derived with the same approach. Regardless that constant values were taken, it isn't supposed to mean that the procedure is an absolute truth. So, in physical sciences it must also carry the dilemma of whether the void exists or not. It is, therefore, evident that mathematics alone could never declare the whole pure absolute truth.

Going back to Figure 2, the radius **Ac** of the circle is the lifeline domain of universal operations and the microcosm respectively with the extended part **ABC** as the most obvious physical microcosm and macrocosm reality that we assumed or saw through physical perception with human instruments and the naked eye. The radius **Ac** could represent the distance of orbital(s) like electrons of the atom (microcosm) or the (radius **AB** in macrocosm) planets with respect to the sun or solar system with respect to the galaxy it belongs to or point **A** as the center of the universe and orbitant **B** in the outskirt domain the universal operations. The circumference of the circle, therefore, with respect to its radius **Ac** is mostly the resultant force between incoming pull/push point **C** and the outgoing force point **B** (interaction of material force and immaterial force). With respect to the solar system, point **B** is the radiation force of light form the sun, while **C** is the gravitational force. The r(s) equals mostly the resultant force utilized by planetary orbits. The only possible way upon which these relationships could be broken or interrupted is when a catastrophic phenomenon would occur with the nucleus of the atom or the sun or when outside forces are exerted against them is strong enough. When the lifeline is broken, life on Earth as we know it will end because force **AB** or **AC** would then be allowed to move toward their maximum potentials (like an energy-consuming black hole). But modern science, through the Hubble telescope in space, had witnessed that in the astronomical domain, young stars are emerging while others seem to be on the verge of destruction. These universal phenomena are representative that line **AB** and **AC** could never be allowed to reach infinity and cease to be an energy or absolute zero value respectively. This theory is relevant to the theory of the conservation of energy. The general operation of reality, therefore, is that all energy is a motion within motions operating according to the principle of the domain of lifelines (radius between points of energy from the smallest even with the energies not seen by human instruments to be the biggest) written in the span of space of the void with a purpose so that straight line would never be possible (refer to the theory of relativity by Einstein with its definition of *energy*. Regardless that it tends to be possible, the void or nothing would never allow it, not unless there would be a need for a universal recreation if humanity (or only to specific persons) would never be allowed to participate in the immortal dimension of reality.

The theory of the black hole, therefore, must only be allowed the domain of its proposition of reality, but perhaps it could be utilized dependent upon the direction of human destiny. So, if there's a creator or God, then He wouldn't be left out without a complete recourse to whatever he deems to do. The human immortal future might be dependent upon how reality is truly interpreted or perceived. The study of Christism has provided such a bilateral or holistic interpretation as an attempt for humanity to have an alternative approach for human salvation or immortal destiny.

It is completely clear that the definition of energy by the theory of relativity $E=mc^2$ (as the most viable assumed human perception with the nature of energy or force). A scientific experiment in human laboratory confirmed that an electron could gain mass in particle accelerators. This experiment expressed reversibility of the theory of relativity so that even if the electron could still be broken apart, the energy expended in the process would be reconverted immediately into smaller mass energy quotients, even to fractions where no human instrument could possibly detect. In simple analysis, absolute zero or void could no longer be attended because it's already full with no vacancy because its domain became infinity so that infinity is already available. The zero immaterial force, therefore, will reject anything added to it because there's no more room. However, because the zero force is itself a force, regardless that it's immaterial and invisible, its force is interlaced with the smallest possible mass of energy, and the argument follows with the biggest possible universal energy or body. To draw a line between the assumed or material or visible energy or mass to the human eye aided with the best of instruments or naked and the unseen immaterial force is not just possible. The whole universal reality, therefore, is self-sustaining and self-preserving for the reason that the immaterial and material forces are distinct from the other; they are one inseparable. We could say, therefore, that reality is not by assumption only, and the existence of the void is evidence of the fact that a human couldn't see or verify it with the naked eye or aided with the best of human instruments.

The existence of a creator or God depends on the theory presented in this study, and as with the advocacy of the study of Christism, the universe is alive as life on planet Earth bears witness. Because the universal material force is alive, so must the immaterial force—described in the study of Christism as God the Father. All religious concepts of immortality depend completely on the basis of the law of conservation of energy, and it's only possible because the void wouldn't allow energy to be destroyed because there's no more room for destruction but only for the instance or recreation which is a contingent momentary event by means of the method of the deity as a complete re-transformation of themselves.

There might be a great danger if science would try to simulate the creation of the universe. Going into the boundary of void and matter could be completely catastrophic within the human existence of domain because we never know how God will react. Human experiments don't necessarily go to the center of the universe to deal with the question of infinity or origin, but the point of universal origin could be within the atom itself and/or with the smallest energy particles themselves.

This study, therefore, suggested that mathematics is not an exact science and never will be because its specific domain is completely only within human material instrumentations recognition and mostly not immune from the proposition of the existence of a creator or God. Although, all the things we are, calculate, and cherish that we see with our naked eye or aided with the most advanced human instruments are as actual and real as the consciousness of matter that the great creator has privileged to us. But the thing unseen and immaterial hasn't been created, but the embodiment of the creator himself must also be given due mutual recognition because it's impossible to believe that the universe is holding itself in space, neither that any attributes with materiality—even if it's invisible to human eye or instruments—of the nature of space could answer the question of what is the nature of infinity. It's the very reason that physical science speculates that the nature of space is an unseen immaterial defies all scientific or religious conventions of truth of the nature of the universe, and the proposition of the actual existence of a purpose, God, or creator couldn't be denied.

In Figure 2 behind the innermost region of point **A** (as well as to the outermost [infinity/void] of point **B**) as the origin (void) is holding and sustaining the whole universal operation domain of *r=ac* with a method that point **C** could never reach an absolute zero energy value; likewise point **B** could never reach infinity. If point **C** and **B** are allowed to reach to their absolute values, then straight lines become possible, and energy could be destroyed. Therefore, all the propositions of immortality become vain. But according to this study of Christism, it will never be possible, not unless by the will of the creator. Because mathematics is a branch of physical sciences, all its mathematical values are assumed physical realities. And obviously, it allowed the proposition of the destruction of energy by which energy defined by material instruments and beyond human instruments are no longer an assumed reality but the end of energy.

But if energy or force could be destroyed into eternal oblivion, then what proposition could be given to answer the nature of infinity? Simultaneously, what is holding the huge universal mass in space? And also, if energy or force could be destroyed, why did it exist in the first place? The only proposition that could answer these questions is to accept the existence of the force of the void, which is the very basis of all universal material existence that humans could recognize or assume. We could never assume or understand the nature of the force of the void because it's beyond the limit of human assumptions and knowledge. Although, we could believe it by faith, there's no possibility whatsoever leading to its understanding.

The argument that mathematics could not declare absolute truth also applies to the mathematical expression **1+2=3**. This mathematical expression couldn't declare an absolute truth regardless that it is mathematically true. But it's nothing but an assumption due to the fact that an indivisible value of **1** is not possible. The expression **1+2=3** could only be regarded as an absolute truth when the availability of an indivisible amount of energy is present that could exist and sustain itself independently. Then and only then that I could be given an absolute value. But such a condition is not possible, for the fact that the universe couldn't possibly hold itself in space. Therefore, the same principle applies that no mathematical expression could express absolute truth without recognizing that the space or void has an immaterial force that is holding the universe(s) in space, and its force is interlaced with the smallest matter or energy as well as with the biggest one. The continuous motion of energy, therefore, is cyclical from near absolute zero to near infinity and vice versa. It's the basis that matter or energy and the universal or atomic motions are curved for the fact that the force of void is always at interplay to prevent any absolute destruction of energy, so the last point of energy division or tendency to destruction is the beginning of recreation of energy to make possible that the most rudimentary elements for the recreation of bigger energy mass is always available. The distinction between the end of the end and the beginning of the beginning is always inconspicuous to human perception, even when aided with his best material instrumentations.

Although, the mathematical expression **1+2=3** is completely mathematically admissible and true, it's nothing but an assumption. But existence is not by assumption only. It requires the argument of faith for the existence of immaterial force or God the creator so that the greatest human dilemma could have a solution and hope, because the absolute truth is with God the father.

197

Notunol: A Study of Christism

by Mac R. Cabanilla

Inks & Bindings

book review by Boze Herrington

"Any act of righteousness, be it of the obedience of law of government or religion, if it's rendered for the law couldn't merit salvation."

Cabanilla lobbies for a reconciliation between science and faith, arguing that the purely materialistic view of the cosmos is limited because it can't explain the existence of beings capable of rational thought. Mere matter, in his estimation, could never contemplate itself. Crucial to his understanding is a belief that Christianity, while the noblest system of religion on offer, needs to adapt itself in response to recent advances in scientific learning if it hopes to maintain adherents in the modern age.

The author's doctrine of "Christism" posits itself as a more enlightened version of traditional Christianity. God the Father in this system is best understood as the void or nothing out of which the universe was created at the beginning of time. God the Son is the material cosmos who seeks to make himself known in self-revelation to existing creatures. The goal towards which all human beings are striving isn't, as some faith traditions have asserted, a perpetual disembodied existence in a heavenly realm but physical immortality within this dimension of time and space. Though Cabanilla is adamant that there remains only one absolute truth rather than a plethora of competing truths, he thinks people differ in their capacity to receive and understand truth, which is why the different religions are necessary. He puts forward the teachings of Christism not as a rival to existing faith traditions but in the hopes that people will better understand their purpose in the world, which is to believe in God and obtain immortality through that belief. He speaks approvingly of Jesus, St. Paul, and Martin Luther, whom he believes were trying to convey this essential truth according to the light that they had. Cabanilla takes pains to assure readers that they can "upgrade" their current faith by embracing Christism without fear of losing their salvation in the tradition they currently practice. Despite the often scientific-sounding jargon with which he presents his tenets, he's merely putting a new gloss on long-existing beliefs.

Cabanilla's curiosity and willingness to reconsider the meaning of basic Christian doctrines are commendable. Jungian psychologist Edward Edinger wrote that some souls are "hermetic," meaning they feel a keen hunger for hidden or esoteric forms of knowledge. In his willingness to defy received opinion in pursuit of a deeper revelation, Cabanilla follows in the steps of the medieval alchemists, Giordano Bruno, and Jung himself. His theory that marriage is a symbolic representation of the cosmic union between spirit and matter evokes the Kabbalistic teaching about the Garden of Pomegranates mentioned in the Song of Songs. There are moments when the book reads like an extended riff on Madeleine L'Engle's Wrinkle in Time quartet, with its daring fusion of science and religion and veneration for previous explorers in the realm of the spirit.

Although the book might upset the incurious, there's little here to offend genuine seekers of wisdom. One could quibble with the notion that rabbinic Judaism was "racist" and that Paul was the first Jew to declare God's love for people of all nations. In fact, Judaism has always maintained that non-Jews can have a relationship with God, and that, in the words of the Talmud, "The righteous of all nations have a share in the world to come." Cabanilla is on firmer ground when he describes the mysterious, ineffable nature of God as depicted in the Bible. He also astutely notes the difficulty of reconciling the portrayal of God in the Hebrew scriptures with the portrayal of God in the New Testament, acknowledging that there are subtle differences in theme and emphasis. The book is a thrilling read for anyone who is spiritually adventurous and willing to have their understanding of faith challenged. Though Cabanilla's language takes some getting used to, there are pearls to be gleaned for those who commit to the journey.

 **Customer Reviews**

Piaras VINE VOICE

★★★★

An insightful and thought-provoking book.
Reviewed in the United States on March 4, 2023
Verified Purchase

"Notunol: A Study of Christism" is an intriguing and thought-provoking book that explores the concept of Christism and its role in shaping our understanding of Christianity. The author takes a unique approach to this subject by delving into the origins and development of Christism, a term he uses to describe the specific interpretations of the life and teachings of Jesus Christ that have emerged over time.

One of the book's main strengths is the author's in-depth analysis of the different forms of Christism that have arisen throughout history, from the early Christian church to contemporary interpretations. Cabanilla explores the ways in which these different interpretations have influenced the way we understand Christ and Christianity, and he provides a comprehensive overview of the various debates and controversies that have arisen as a result.

Another strength of the book is Cabanilla's willingness to challenge conventional wisdom and explore alternative perspectives on Christianity. He argues that many of the beliefs and practices that are commonly associated with Christianity today are actually the result of later interpretations and cultural influences, rather than being inherent to the faith itself. This approach allows the reader to question their own assumptions and to consider new ways of thinking about this important religious tradition.

While the book is well-researched and informative, it is also accessible and engaging to a general audience. Cabanilla's writing is clear and concise, and he uses real-world examples and anecdotes to illustrate his points. He also includes helpful summaries and definitions throughout the book, making it easy for readers to follow along and understand the complex ideas he presents.

"Notunol: A Study of Christism" is an insightful and thought-provoking book that offers a fresh perspective on the history and meaning of Christianity. Whether you are a devout Christian or simply interested in the history of religion, this book is sure to provide valuable insights and stimulate new ideas.

Grady Harp

A quiet and sensitive exploration of the meaning of existence
Reviewed in the United States on March 5, 2023
Verified Purchase

Philippine-born Hawaii author Mac R. Cabanilla pens his debut book with a compassionate, caring, and meaningful collection of musings about the nature of existence. He opens with the following, 'The preservation of all living organisms completely depends on the faithful observance of the structure of morality inherently provided by Creator or God.' He develops his concept of 'Christism' well: 'a unified concept that ties together mankind, the Holy Spirit, and the nature of the universe.' Explaining Christism and Notunol (the Nature of Life), he offers a blend of universal truth and faith as a combination of physical reality and immaterial forces, or faith in the spiritual realm of God. As he states, 'Existence is not by assumption only. It requires the argument of faith for the existence of immaterial force or God the creator so that the greatest human dilemma could have a solution and hope, because the absolute truth is with God the father.' This is a well-written book that offers explanations of understanding faith, religion, and philosophy.

Primer

Enlightening
Reviewed in the United States on March 9, 2023
Verified Purchase

Mac R. Cabanilla's debut novel is nothing short of profound. Deep does this freshman author delve into the universal question of why we are who we are? I believe that Cabanilla's writing is the complete opposite of what existentialists believe. This novel painstakingly discusses the basic principles that determine how people partake in worshipping a superior being, God, and how they strive to find a deeper meaning to their own existence. The book brings out individuals' perceptions, their noticing of, and quite often partaking in the beauties of all that surrounds us. It is the mixing together of the gifts God has bestowed upon His people and, in turn, those people's responses to Him. The nature of the universe and the nature of life--Notunol--is the root concept from which Cabanilla draws his arguments. As discussed at length, the philosophies can become burdensome and even times obfuscated to the average reader. The book is for those with a keen sense of wonderment on this specific topic, with a deep yearning to expand their thinking and their understanding, to embrace the logic of life, and their enlightenment through God.

Ghulam Mustafa

Learn more about life & existence.
Reviewed in the United States on March 9, 2023
Verified Purchase

Notunol: A Study of Christism by Mac R Cabanilla presents an in-depth exploration of the nature of religious belief, examining the fundamental tenets that govern how people practice faith and find meaning in their lives. The book delves into Notunol, a concept that suggests there is more to life than simply living to make it through to the afterlife. It proposes that understanding our world and the universe around us offer greater insight into what comes next.

At its core, *Notunol* suggests there are deeper truths underlying our existence, ones that must be embraced if we are to have any understanding at all. By exploring Notunol, this book offers readers an opportunity to explore these ideas further, giving them a better understanding of what faith entails beyond what is typically expressed by major religions.

This comprehensive examination provides both experienced and new believers alike with food for thought on how they can approach their beliefs from different angles and uncover nuances and complexities previously unknown. If you are curious about religion and the possibilities it may offer, then this book is a must-read.

Phil Bolos

Notunol may be the missing piece of faith
Reviewed in the United States on March 5, 2023
Verified Purchase

Notunol: A Study of Christism by Mac R Cabanilla takes the reader on an extensive look into what it means to be religious, the key themes or ideas behind religions and religious beliefs, and finally looks at Notunol (the nature of the universe and the nature of life). All major religions expect followers to believe that there is an afterlife and a path or set of expectations that must be followed in order to reach that afterlife and the deity that holds power there. But, what if there was more to it than that? What if there was an understanding with all the surrounds us that must be met for us t even have a slight understanding of what comes next? That is where Notunol comes in. The author does a great job of explaining what this new idea is and how it fits into the bigger picture of faith and belief. If you question religion or wonder if there is more to faith than what major religions present, then this is a great book for you.

Ivan

Interesting point of view.
Reviewed in the United States on March 9, 2023
Verified Purchase

Notunol: A Study of Christism is a complete study of religion, nature, and humanity, written by Mac R. Cabanilla. I don't consider myself a religious person, even though I believe in a superior being. This book takes a different angle on the subject, it's not the classic book that spreads the word of god, and that's why I like it.

There's so much more in the world besides organized religion, we as humans have been around for a few thousands of years, and we share with every living organism the same characteristics in so many aspects that I couldn't believe it when I read it.

Overall, a book destined for readers who want to challenge their beliefs and give a tour throughout history!

Nela

Challenging and attractive
Reviewed in the United States on March 10, 2023
Verified Purchase

Notunol by author Mac R. Cabanilla is a deep study of Christism, where the revision of the nature of life, of God and of faith is carried out, delving into the interrelationships between the material, the immaterial, and the spiritual; with the final aim to understand the nature of the universe and the nature of life. I think this is an intricate but challenging approach and attractive for interested readers. It is a thought-provoking and comprehensive perspective on the subject that will surely have many followers.

Abdullah

Exploration of the concept of faith that challenges traditional religious beliefs.
Reviewed in the United States on March 14, 2023
Verified Purchase

"Notunol: A Study of Christism" is a book by Mac R. Cabanilla that delves into the concept of faith and its relationship with the nature of the universe and life.

The book proposes an intriguing idea that having faith entails more than simply accepting the existence of a higher power and leading a morally reputable life. It involves comprehending the interconnectedness among the tangible, intangible, and divine domains.

Overall, this study presents a fascinating exploration of the concept of faith that challenges traditional religious beliefs.

Momna

A must-read if you are looking for a different perspective!
Reviewed in the United States on March 8, 2023
Verified Purchase

Religions all over the world have established beliefs that generally include the concept of a Supreme power, an afterlife, and a philosophy on the importance of existence. Mac R. Cabanilla's "Notunol: A Study of Christism" is an in-depth exploration of the nature of life, God, and faith. The author presents a convincing argument that the ultimate goal of faith or religion is to understand the complex interconnections between the material, immaterial, and spiritual aspects of the universe.

A must-read if you are looking for a different perspective!

Marina Lujan

An interesting book!
Reviewed in the United States on March 11, 2023
Verified Purchase

The excellent book *Notunol* questions the widely held belief that having a Christian faith merely entails subscribing to a set of religious doctrines. I get the impression that this book is approachable for all readers while also being challenging and inspiring.

Your existing beliefs may be questioned and you may find yourself reflecting after reading this book. The author's explanations and arguments are clear and convincing, making the book highly recommended for those who wish to deepen their faith.

Hassan

A must-read if have an open mind and can read and understand other people›s viewpoints.
Reviewed in the United States on March 8, 2023
Verified Purchase

In his book, "Notunol: A Study of Christism," Mac R. Cabanilla explores the concept of Christism, which he presents as a unified belief system that extends beyond mere adherence to a religious doctrine. The author discusses that true faith confines a deep understanding of the interconnections between material, immaterial, and spiritual realms.

The book is not for everyone, but if you have an open mind and can read and understand other people's viewpoints then you must read this book.

Nicki

A Discourse on Humanity, Religion, and Morality
Reviewed in the United States on March 11, 2023
Verified Purchase

The book discusses on a number of things, including sin, morality, laws, and how the mankind is increasingly getting monatized and diverting from its real purpose. It explores the history of the earth along with the history of manking and talks about the different makeup of man from that of the animal kingdom, despite sharing the same geneology. To conclude, it makes an intelligent discourse on numerous topics centered around man, sins, morality, and law, and introduces the readers to many new concepts and words.

Conscientious

Interesting and unique.
Reviewed in the United States on March 11, 2023
Verified Purchase

Notunol by R Cabanilla, Mac is an enlightening book paving way to understanding the way to religious faith is beyond a set of religious beliefs and must encompass a unified concept. Man must come to understand the various interrelationships and hence will understand the nature of the universe and the nature of life. The author is straightforward and presents a wide world of concepts to explore. Overall, an interesting read to stimulate the thought process and expand mind space.

S. J. Main

An interesting religious book.
Reviewed in the United States on March 18, 2023
Verified Purchase

'Notunol' is a self-help religious book written purely about faith, God, belief and the understanding behind it all. It is written well and to the point. I liked how organized it was. If you like to read religious material, then you will find this book attractive to read.